BASIC MATH DRILLS

3rd Grade Mixed Problems

{TIMED TEST}

SPI MATH
WORKBOOKS

ISBN-13:
978-1722454111

ISBN-10:
1722454113

$7\overline{)49}$ $\begin{array}{r} 6 \\ \times\ 8 \\ \hline \end{array}$ $\begin{array}{r} 12 \\ -\ 6 \\ \hline \end{array}$ $\begin{array}{r} 8 \\ \times\ 1 \\ \hline \end{array}$ $\begin{array}{r} 6 \\ +\ 2 \\ \hline \end{array}$ $\begin{array}{r} 2 \\ \times\ 5 \\ \hline \end{array}$ $\begin{array}{r} 1 \\ \times\ 4 \\ \hline \end{array}$ $\begin{array}{r} 5 \\ \times\ 5 \\ \hline \end{array}$ $\begin{array}{r} 4 \\ -\ 3 \\ \hline \end{array}$

$\begin{array}{r} 11 \\ -\ 5 \\ \hline \end{array}$ $\begin{array}{r} 7 \\ +\ 9 \\ \hline \end{array}$ $6\overline{)24}$ $5\overline{)20}$ $\begin{array}{r} 6 \\ \times\ 5 \\ \hline \end{array}$ $\begin{array}{r} 3 \\ +\ 5 \\ \hline \end{array}$ $\begin{array}{r} 8 \\ \times\ 8 \\ \hline \end{array}$ $2\overline{)12}$ $\begin{array}{r} 1 \\ \times\ 3 \\ \hline \end{array}$

$\begin{array}{r} 12 \\ -\ 3 \\ \hline \end{array}$ $4\overline{)24}$ $\begin{array}{r} 8 \\ -\ 1 \\ \hline \end{array}$ $7\overline{)21}$ $\begin{array}{r} 13 \\ -\ 7 \\ \hline \end{array}$ $\begin{array}{r} 1 \\ +\ 4 \\ \hline \end{array}$ $8\overline{)48}$ $\begin{array}{r} 4 \\ +\ 5 \\ \hline \end{array}$ $\begin{array}{r} 3 \\ -\ 2 \\ \hline \end{array}$

$\begin{array}{r} 16 \\ -\ 9 \\ \hline \end{array}$ $\begin{array}{r} 7 \\ +\ 6 \\ \hline \end{array}$ $4\overline{)28}$ $\begin{array}{r} 1 \\ \times\ 8 \\ \hline \end{array}$ $\begin{array}{r} 5 \\ \times\ 8 \\ \hline \end{array}$ $5\overline{)5}$ $\begin{array}{r} 3 \\ \times\ 7 \\ \hline \end{array}$ $\begin{array}{r} 6 \\ -\ 3 \\ \hline \end{array}$ $\begin{array}{r} 5 \\ \times\ 9 \\ \hline \end{array}$

$\begin{array}{r} 9 \\ +\ 5 \\ \hline \end{array}$ $\begin{array}{r} 14 \\ -\ 7 \\ \hline \end{array}$ $\begin{array}{r} 7 \\ -\ 4 \\ \hline \end{array}$ $9\overline{)54}$ $\begin{array}{r} 3 \\ \times\ 3 \\ \hline \end{array}$ $\begin{array}{r} 1 \\ \times\ 2 \\ \hline \end{array}$ $\begin{array}{r} 5 \\ \times\ 6 \\ \hline \end{array}$ $\begin{array}{r} 8 \\ +\ 1 \\ \hline \end{array}$ $5\overline{)35}$

$\begin{array}{r} 1 \\ +\ 1 \\ \hline \end{array}$ $\begin{array}{r} 5 \\ +\ 1 \\ \hline \end{array}$ $\begin{array}{r} 7 \\ \times\ 1 \\ \hline \end{array}$ $\begin{array}{r} 4 \\ \times\ 1 \\ \hline \end{array}$ $\begin{array}{r} 7 \\ -\ 1 \\ \hline \end{array}$ $\begin{array}{r} 8 \\ +\ 2 \\ \hline \end{array}$ $\begin{array}{r} 7 \\ -\ 6 \\ \hline \end{array}$ $5\overline{)10}$ $\begin{array}{r} 3 \\ -\ 1 \\ \hline \end{array}$

$\begin{array}{r} 3 \\ \times\ 8 \\ \hline \end{array}$ $\begin{array}{r} 7 \\ +\ 2 \\ \hline \end{array}$ $\begin{array}{r} 6 \\ +\ 3 \\ \hline \end{array}$ $\begin{array}{r} 8 \\ -\ 7 \\ \hline \end{array}$ $\begin{array}{r} 5 \\ +\ 7 \\ \hline \end{array}$ $\begin{array}{r} 14 \\ -\ 5 \\ \hline \end{array}$ $\begin{array}{r} 9 \\ +\ 6 \\ \hline \end{array}$ $\begin{array}{r} 13 \\ -\ 9 \\ \hline \end{array}$ $\begin{array}{r} 5 \\ \times\ 7 \\ \hline \end{array}$

$\begin{array}{r} 6 \\ +\ 8 \\ \hline \end{array}$ $\begin{array}{r} 17 \\ -\ 9 \\ \hline \end{array}$ $\begin{array}{r} 14 \\ -\ 9 \\ \hline \end{array}$ $\begin{array}{r} 10 \\ -\ 6 \\ \hline \end{array}$ $\begin{array}{r} 12 \\ -\ 7 \\ \hline \end{array}$ $\begin{array}{r} 9 \\ \times\ 6 \\ \hline \end{array}$ $\begin{array}{r} 3 \\ \times\ 9 \\ \hline \end{array}$ $1\overline{)6}$ $\begin{array}{r} 2 \\ +\ 2 \\ \hline \end{array}$

$\begin{array}{r} 9 \\ \times\ 4 \\ \hline \end{array}$ $\begin{array}{r} 7 \\ -\ 2 \\ \hline \end{array}$ $\begin{array}{r} 8 \\ \times\ 6 \\ \hline \end{array}$ $8\overline{)40}$ $1\overline{)4}$ $\begin{array}{r} 15 \\ -\ 6 \\ \hline \end{array}$ $\begin{array}{r} 11 \\ -\ 4 \\ \hline \end{array}$ $\begin{array}{r} 2 \\ +\ 6 \\ \hline \end{array}$ $6\overline{)18}$

14 − 5	6 − 5	9 + 3	2 × 4	1 + 5	9 × 8	7 − 5	1)5	3 × 7
3)3	6 + 4	5 × 4	2)12	9)72	6 + 3	5 × 2	6)36	4 − 2
3 + 2	8)32	5 + 6	2)6	9)9	7 − 6	4 + 3	4 + 1	8 × 1
4 + 4	1)3	4 + 8	6 + 1	1 + 2	5 + 9	8 + 5	16 − 8	10 − 1
9)81	10 − 3	3 − 2	7)63	9 + 9	4)20	9)18	2 + 9	2 × 3
7 + 5	8 + 9	2 + 3	9 × 3	3 × 5	2 × 5	9 − 4	1)4	11 − 8
8 + 1	7)28	12 − 4	1)6	1 + 6	2)10	8)8	16 − 7	5)30
3 + 7	4)32	4 × 8	2 + 1	2)4	6)18	2)14	2 × 6	8 − 5
5)15	7 × 4	3 × 2	14 − 8	2 × 1	4 × 2	6)42	3)12	5 + 5

$$\begin{array}{r} 7 \\ +\ 5 \\ \hline \end{array} \qquad 5\overline{)15} \qquad \begin{array}{r} 6 \\ \times\ 3 \\ \hline \end{array} \qquad \begin{array}{r} 8 \\ +\ 7 \\ \hline \end{array} \qquad \begin{array}{r} 8 \\ -\ 4 \\ \hline \end{array} \qquad 9\overline{)81} \qquad \begin{array}{r} 6 \\ -\ 1 \\ \hline \end{array} \qquad \begin{array}{r} 9 \\ +\ 5 \\ \hline \end{array} \qquad \begin{array}{r} 9 \\ -\ 5 \\ \hline \end{array}$$

$$\begin{array}{r} 5 \\ \times\ 1 \\ \hline \end{array} \qquad \begin{array}{r} 15 \\ -\ 9 \\ \hline \end{array} \qquad \begin{array}{r} 5 \\ +\ 2 \\ \hline \end{array} \qquad \begin{array}{r} 1 \\ +\ 6 \\ \hline \end{array} \qquad \begin{array}{r} 1 \\ +\ 3 \\ \hline \end{array} \qquad \begin{array}{r} 10 \\ -\ 6 \\ \hline \end{array} \qquad \begin{array}{r} 9 \\ -\ 8 \\ \hline \end{array} \qquad 7\overline{)56} \qquad \begin{array}{r} 2 \\ \times\ 5 \\ \hline \end{array}$$

$$\begin{array}{r} 12 \\ -\ 7 \\ \hline \end{array} \qquad \begin{array}{r} 5 \\ +\ 8 \\ \hline \end{array} \qquad \begin{array}{r} 2 \\ \times\ 4 \\ \hline \end{array} \qquad \begin{array}{r} 11 \\ -\ 5 \\ \hline \end{array} \qquad \begin{array}{r} 6 \\ \times\ 7 \\ \hline \end{array} \qquad \begin{array}{r} 1 \\ \times\ 9 \\ \hline \end{array} \qquad 1\overline{)1} \qquad 4\overline{)36} \qquad \begin{array}{r} 11 \\ -\ 4 \\ \hline \end{array}$$

$$7\overline{)42} \qquad 2\overline{)8} \qquad 6\overline{)54} \qquad \begin{array}{r} 9 \\ +\ 6 \\ \hline \end{array} \qquad \begin{array}{r} 10 \\ -\ 3 \\ \hline \end{array} \qquad 4\overline{)28} \qquad \begin{array}{r} 6 \\ \times\ 5 \\ \hline \end{array} \qquad \begin{array}{r} 14 \\ -\ 5 \\ \hline \end{array} \qquad \begin{array}{r} 7 \\ \times\ 6 \\ \hline \end{array}$$

$$\begin{array}{r} 4 \\ +\ 4 \\ \hline \end{array} \qquad \begin{array}{r} 8 \\ \times\ 5 \\ \hline \end{array} \qquad \begin{array}{r} 3 \\ +\ 8 \\ \hline \end{array} \qquad \begin{array}{r} 6 \\ +\ 5 \\ \hline \end{array} \qquad 7\overline{)49} \qquad \begin{array}{r} 5 \\ +\ 6 \\ \hline \end{array} \qquad \begin{array}{r} 12 \\ -\ 5 \\ \hline \end{array} \qquad \begin{array}{r} 13 \\ -\ 6 \\ \hline \end{array} \qquad \begin{array}{r} 8 \\ \times\ 7 \\ \hline \end{array}$$

$$\begin{array}{r} 8 \\ \times\ 6 \\ \hline \end{array} \qquad \begin{array}{r} 11 \\ -\ 2 \\ \hline \end{array} \qquad \begin{array}{r} 7 \\ +\ 6 \\ \hline \end{array} \qquad 9\overline{)27} \qquad \begin{array}{r} 8 \\ +\ 4 \\ \hline \end{array} \qquad \begin{array}{r} 5 \\ -\ 1 \\ \hline \end{array} \qquad 9\overline{)36} \qquad \begin{array}{r} 7 \\ +\ 7 \\ \hline \end{array} \qquad \begin{array}{r} 9 \\ -\ 4 \\ \hline \end{array}$$

$$\begin{array}{r} 6 \\ \times\ 4 \\ \hline \end{array} \qquad 5\overline{)30} \qquad \begin{array}{r} 3 \\ +\ 7 \\ \hline \end{array} \qquad \begin{array}{r} 7 \\ \times\ 5 \\ \hline \end{array} \qquad 6\overline{)36} \qquad \begin{array}{r} 4 \\ -\ 3 \\ \hline \end{array} \qquad 7\overline{)63} \qquad 9\overline{)54} \qquad \begin{array}{r} 7 \\ -\ 5 \\ \hline \end{array}$$

$$8\overline{)40} \qquad 1\overline{)7} \qquad \begin{array}{r} 6 \\ \times\ 6 \\ \hline \end{array} \qquad 7\overline{)7} \qquad 9\overline{)72} \qquad \begin{array}{r} 9 \\ \times\ 8 \\ \hline \end{array} \qquad \begin{array}{r} 7 \\ +\ 1 \\ \hline \end{array} \qquad 8\overline{)64} \qquad \begin{array}{r} 8 \\ +\ 9 \\ \hline \end{array}$$

$$7\overline{)35} \qquad \begin{array}{r} 1 \\ +\ 8 \\ \hline \end{array} \qquad \begin{array}{r} 2 \\ \times\ 1 \\ \hline \end{array} \qquad \begin{array}{r} 7 \\ -\ 2 \\ \hline \end{array} \qquad \begin{array}{r} 5 \\ \times\ 6 \\ \hline \end{array} \qquad \begin{array}{r} 6 \\ +\ 8 \\ \hline \end{array} \qquad 5\overline{)10} \qquad 3\overline{)12} \qquad \begin{array}{r} 3 \\ \times\ 1 \\ \hline \end{array}$$

3 + 3	13 - 5	5 × 9	5 × 6	8 + 8	3 × 2	7)14	7 + 4	4)28
6 + 7	5 × 7	8 + 9	7)49	8 × 7	8 + 6	8 × 3	9 - 5	4 - 3
6 + 6	2)18	5 + 9	14 - 6	4 + 7	10 - 1	7)28	3)9	2)6
4 + 1	7)35	6 - 5	2 - 1	3 × 6	2 × 2	9 - 3	17 - 9	3 + 9
5 + 8	6 - 1	8)72	3 - 1	1 × 6	7 × 2	7 + 5	4 + 2	5 + 7
1 + 1	5)15	2 + 8	9 + 6	6 + 5	3 + 2	3 × 5	6 × 1	9 - 1
2 + 1	4 × 1	3 + 5	9 × 7	8 × 8	12 - 3	8 + 1	10 - 3	2 + 3
2)12	4 × 8	15 - 7	9 - 7	5 - 4	5 + 4	6 - 4	4 + 4	9 × 1
2 × 6	2)2	4)24	16 - 7	6 × 2	5 - 3	15 - 8	9 - 6	4 + 5

$6\overline{)42}$	$\begin{array}{r}4\\ \times\ 1\\\hline\end{array}$	$6\overline{)18}$	$3\overline{)27}$	$\begin{array}{r}5\\ +\ 5\\\hline\end{array}$	$\begin{array}{r}6\\ -\ 5\\\hline\end{array}$	$\begin{array}{r}1\\ +\ 6\\\hline\end{array}$	$\begin{array}{r}6\\ \times\ 9\\\hline\end{array}$	$2\overline{)14}$
$\begin{array}{r}10\\ -\ 3\\\hline\end{array}$	$\begin{array}{r}11\\ -\ 2\\\hline\end{array}$	$\begin{array}{r}7\\ +\ 2\\\hline\end{array}$	$\begin{array}{r}9\\ +\ 2\\\hline\end{array}$	$\begin{array}{r}5\\ +\ 1\\\hline\end{array}$	$1\overline{)5}$	$\begin{array}{r}5\\ \times\ 6\\\hline\end{array}$	$\begin{array}{r}8\\ -\ 6\\\hline\end{array}$	$\begin{array}{r}6\\ +\ 3\\\hline\end{array}$
$\begin{array}{r}3\\ +\ 2\\\hline\end{array}$	$\begin{array}{r}4\\ -\ 1\\\hline\end{array}$	$\begin{array}{r}1\\ +\ 2\\\hline\end{array}$	$\begin{array}{r}3\\ +\ 4\\\hline\end{array}$	$\begin{array}{r}4\\ \times\ 2\\\hline\end{array}$	$\begin{array}{r}9\\ \times\ 3\\\hline\end{array}$	$\begin{array}{r}8\\ \times\ 5\\\hline\end{array}$	$\begin{array}{r}3\\ \times\ 5\\\hline\end{array}$	$7\overline{)56}$
$6\overline{)36}$	$\begin{array}{r}12\\ -\ 5\\\hline\end{array}$	$9\overline{)27}$	$\begin{array}{r}1\\ +\ 4\\\hline\end{array}$	$\begin{array}{r}5\\ \times\ 9\\\hline\end{array}$	$\begin{array}{r}9\\ \times\ 2\\\hline\end{array}$	$\begin{array}{r}7\\ +\ 6\\\hline\end{array}$	$9\overline{)72}$	$\begin{array}{r}9\\ \times\ 1\\\hline\end{array}$
$\begin{array}{r}1\\ +\ 8\\\hline\end{array}$	$\begin{array}{r}7\\ +\ 7\\\hline\end{array}$	$\begin{array}{r}2\\ +\ 1\\\hline\end{array}$	$\begin{array}{r}5\\ \times\ 3\\\hline\end{array}$	$\begin{array}{r}14\\ -\ 6\\\hline\end{array}$	$\begin{array}{r}2\\ \times\ 3\\\hline\end{array}$	$\begin{array}{r}6\\ +\ 9\\\hline\end{array}$	$\begin{array}{r}11\\ -\ 6\\\hline\end{array}$	$\begin{array}{r}7\\ \times\ 1\\\hline\end{array}$
$\begin{array}{r}15\\ -\ 7\\\hline\end{array}$	$\begin{array}{r}3\\ +\ 5\\\hline\end{array}$	$4\overline{)28}$	$\begin{array}{r}8\\ +\ 1\\\hline\end{array}$	$\begin{array}{r}5\\ -\ 2\\\hline\end{array}$	$\begin{array}{r}7\\ -\ 6\\\hline\end{array}$	$\begin{array}{r}7\\ -\ 1\\\hline\end{array}$	$\begin{array}{r}6\\ +\ 8\\\hline\end{array}$	$6\overline{)24}$
$\begin{array}{r}13\\ -\ 5\\\hline\end{array}$	$3\overline{)24}$	$\begin{array}{r}6\\ \times\ 2\\\hline\end{array}$	$\begin{array}{r}7\\ \times\ 3\\\hline\end{array}$	$\begin{array}{r}1\\ +\ 9\\\hline\end{array}$	$\begin{array}{r}6\\ +\ 4\\\hline\end{array}$	$9\overline{)18}$	$3\overline{)18}$	$\begin{array}{r}2\\ \times\ 7\\\hline\end{array}$
$\begin{array}{r}6\\ +\ 2\\\hline\end{array}$	$\begin{array}{r}11\\ -\ 3\\\hline\end{array}$	$\begin{array}{r}9\\ +\ 8\\\hline\end{array}$	$\begin{array}{r}3\\ +\ 1\\\hline\end{array}$	$\begin{array}{r}9\\ -\ 8\\\hline\end{array}$	$\begin{array}{r}9\\ \times\ 4\\\hline\end{array}$	$\begin{array}{r}8\\ \times\ 2\\\hline\end{array}$	$\begin{array}{r}6\\ \times\ 8\\\hline\end{array}$	$\begin{array}{r}15\\ -\ 6\\\hline\end{array}$
$\begin{array}{r}1\\ +\ 5\\\hline\end{array}$	$\begin{array}{r}4\\ +\ 4\\\hline\end{array}$	$\begin{array}{r}2\\ -\ 1\\\hline\end{array}$	$\begin{array}{r}8\\ -\ 5\\\hline\end{array}$	$8\overline{)64}$	$3\overline{)15}$	$\begin{array}{r}12\\ -\ 6\\\hline\end{array}$	$\begin{array}{r}5\\ +\ 7\\\hline\end{array}$	$\begin{array}{r}6\\ \times\ 6\\\hline\end{array}$

Name_____ Date _____ Score _____

4 + 2	15 − 7	8)56	8)16	7 + 1	10 − 1	10 − 7	5)40	9 × 2
2 × 4	1 × 9	8 × 9	8 + 5	9 + 7	5 + 9	9)18	8 − 4	3 × 8
7 × 2	8 + 9	15 − 9	3 × 9	12 − 5	9 + 4	16 − 9	9 × 4	13 − 4
4)8	5 − 4	5 × 7	4 × 1	13 − 5	9 − 8	1 × 2	3 + 6	4 − 3
17 − 9	4)28	7)28	1 × 5	7)56	1)7	3 − 1	2 − 1	7 + 7
9 × 3	1)2	3 × 3	12 − 7	1)9	6 × 4	2)10	3)3	8 × 4
2 × 6	11 − 8	13 − 9	9 × 1	9 + 5	9 + 1	2 × 9	2 × 2	1 + 8
6 − 1	10 − 9	2 + 8	2 × 3	9 × 5	2 + 4	5 + 3	8 − 2	7 + 8
6 + 3	7 × 4	1)3	7)49	4 − 1	7 × 3	5)20	1 × 4	1 + 3

6

Name_____ Date _____ Score _____

```
    6        9        8        8        2        3        2        7        2
  + 9      × 7      - 1      + 9      × 6      × 5      × 5      × 1      - 1


    2        2        9                 8        8        7                10
  + 1      + 9      × 5     1)2       × 7      × 8      - 3     1)5       - 8


   11        3        7        6        1       11        5        3        6
  - 3      × 8      × 7      + 6      × 1      - 5      × 5      × 2      × 1


   10        1        5        8        8        8        2       17        5
  - 5      × 4      + 9      - 3      × 4      - 7      + 2      - 9      × 9


    3        5        7        6                 8        3        9        4
  × 3      + 6      - 1      × 8     4)12       × 9      × 7      + 6      × 7


    9                 7                11                 8        5        9
  - 6     9)81      × 4     5)5       - 8     5)35       × 1      × 8      - 8


    9        4                                   8        3        3        5
  + 2      × 5     1)7     3)21     4)4        × 3      × 4      + 8      × 1


    1                          1       16       14        4        8        6
  × 6     4)20    7)63      + 3      - 8      - 6      + 6      - 2      - 4


    1        7        1        2        5        5       12        9       14
  × 8      + 3      × 3      + 3      + 5      - 1      - 3      - 2      - 8
```

7

10 - 9	8 × 1	7 - 5	4 × 7	10 - 5	3 × 5	9 × 4	2 × 1	7 + 2
3 + 9	7 + 4	1 + 9	4)16	9 - 1	5 + 4	8 × 7	3)9	12 - 3
1 + 4	2)6	9 × 9	6 × 4	7 + 6	4)32	1)7	10 - 2	6)24
2 × 6	9 + 5	9)36	6 × 1	13 - 8	7 × 1	4 + 7	7 × 8	4 + 9
10 - 3	1 + 6	8 - 6	4 × 1	3 × 3	8)64	9 × 1	8 + 4	1)8
7)63	18 - 9	7 + 9	6 - 5	6 - 1	1 + 2	3 + 2	6 × 5	16 - 8
5 + 7	6 - 4	3 + 7	7 × 9	4)20	9 - 3	8 - 4	7 + 8	9 + 8
5)10	1 + 8	9 + 6	2 + 7	4 + 6	6 + 7	1 × 9	4 + 4	5 + 3
9 + 1	7 - 2	2 + 2	2)8	5 × 7	15 - 9	4)36	4 + 2	1)3

8 + 8	2)2	8 + 9	2 × 4	13 - 8	1 + 4	10 - 3	15 - 9	8 + 4
7 + 7	8 × 1	5 + 1	2 + 9	1 × 3	5)15	9 - 3	5)20	15 - 8
6 × 8	5 × 9	9)36	2 - 1	6 - 1	10 - 8	5 + 9	7 - 4	10 - 1
5 × 1	6 + 1	3 × 8	5)35	1)8	2)8	5)40	4 + 8	9 × 3
8 × 9	3)21	1 + 6	3 × 2	14 - 7	9 + 2	9)45	8)16	7 + 8
7)7	4 + 3	7 × 2	1)5	2 × 7	9 × 1	6 × 4	7 - 6	4 × 2
1)6	12 - 6	3)3	7 - 2	2)16	5 - 2	13 - 4	5 - 4	5)45
4 + 1	7 - 3	4 + 7	4)20	8 - 4	11 - 2	5 + 6	15 - 7	9 × 5
9)9	8)24	4 × 3	3 × 5	10 - 9	14 - 9	15 - 6	8 × 8	9 × 6

Row 1:
$\begin{array}{r}5\\ \times\,7\\ \hline\end{array}$ $4\overline{)24}$ $\begin{array}{r}8\\ -\,3\\ \hline\end{array}$ $\begin{array}{r}9\\ \times\,2\\ \hline\end{array}$ $7\overline{)35}$ $\begin{array}{r}3\\ +\,9\\ \hline\end{array}$ $\begin{array}{r}14\\ -\,6\\ \hline\end{array}$ $\begin{array}{r}1\\ +\,8\\ \hline\end{array}$ $3\overline{)27}$

Row 2:
$\begin{array}{r}9\\ -\,2\\ \hline\end{array}$ $\begin{array}{r}6\\ +\,1\\ \hline\end{array}$ $\begin{array}{r}3\\ \times\,4\\ \hline\end{array}$ $\begin{array}{r}3\\ +\,2\\ \hline\end{array}$ $3\overline{)18}$ $\begin{array}{r}7\\ \times\,9\\ \hline\end{array}$ $\begin{array}{r}9\\ \times\,1\\ \hline\end{array}$ $1\overline{)7}$ $4\overline{)16}$

Row 3:
$\begin{array}{r}11\\ -\,2\\ \hline\end{array}$ $4\overline{)12}$ $\begin{array}{r}10\\ -\,6\\ \hline\end{array}$ $\begin{array}{r}6\\ +\,6\\ \hline\end{array}$ $\begin{array}{r}5\\ \times\,5\\ \hline\end{array}$ $\begin{array}{r}13\\ -\,8\\ \hline\end{array}$ $\begin{array}{r}2\\ +\,2\\ \hline\end{array}$ $1\overline{)3}$ $\begin{array}{r}3\\ +\,4\\ \hline\end{array}$

Row 4:
$\begin{array}{r}15\\ -\,9\\ \hline\end{array}$ $7\overline{)63}$ $\begin{array}{r}11\\ -\,5\\ \hline\end{array}$ $\begin{array}{r}4\\ \times\,8\\ \hline\end{array}$ $\begin{array}{r}4\\ \times\,3\\ \hline\end{array}$ $\begin{array}{r}9\\ +\,3\\ \hline\end{array}$ $2\overline{)14}$ $\begin{array}{r}5\\ +\,4\\ \hline\end{array}$ $\begin{array}{r}9\\ +\,7\\ \hline\end{array}$

Row 5:
$\begin{array}{r}6\\ \times\,1\\ \hline\end{array}$ $\begin{array}{r}9\\ \times\,4\\ \hline\end{array}$ $\begin{array}{r}1\\ \times\,7\\ \hline\end{array}$ $3\overline{)21}$ $8\overline{)32}$ $\begin{array}{r}5\\ \times\,2\\ \hline\end{array}$ $\begin{array}{r}2\\ +\,5\\ \hline\end{array}$ $1\overline{)4}$ $\begin{array}{r}10\\ -\,3\\ \hline\end{array}$

Row 6:
$9\overline{)18}$ $\begin{array}{r}7\\ -\,5\\ \hline\end{array}$ $2\overline{)4}$ $\begin{array}{r}16\\ -\,7\\ \hline\end{array}$ $\begin{array}{r}6\\ +\,5\\ \hline\end{array}$ $4\overline{)36}$ $6\overline{)42}$ $\begin{array}{r}8\\ +\,1\\ \hline\end{array}$ $\begin{array}{r}5\\ \times\,6\\ \hline\end{array}$

Row 7:
$\begin{array}{r}1\\ \times\,4\\ \hline\end{array}$ $\begin{array}{r}7\\ -\,6\\ \hline\end{array}$ $\begin{array}{r}5\\ -\,2\\ \hline\end{array}$ $\begin{array}{r}4\\ +\,4\\ \hline\end{array}$ $\begin{array}{r}9\\ \times\,5\\ \hline\end{array}$ $\begin{array}{r}2\\ +\,4\\ \hline\end{array}$ $8\overline{)64}$ $\begin{array}{r}8\\ \times\,2\\ \hline\end{array}$ $9\overline{)9}$

Row 8:
$\begin{array}{r}3\\ -\,2\\ \hline\end{array}$ $\begin{array}{r}4\\ \times\,4\\ \hline\end{array}$ $\begin{array}{r}6\\ +\,4\\ \hline\end{array}$ $\begin{array}{r}4\\ \times\,7\\ \hline\end{array}$ $\begin{array}{r}10\\ -\,4\\ \hline\end{array}$ $3\overline{)9}$ $\begin{array}{r}5\\ \times\,8\\ \hline\end{array}$ $\begin{array}{r}8\\ \times\,7\\ \hline\end{array}$ $\begin{array}{r}4\\ +\,1\\ \hline\end{array}$

Row 9:
$\begin{array}{r}2\\ +\,3\\ \hline\end{array}$ $\begin{array}{r}7\\ +\,9\\ \hline\end{array}$ $\begin{array}{r}5\\ -\,3\\ \hline\end{array}$ $\begin{array}{r}8\\ +\,4\\ \hline\end{array}$ $\begin{array}{r}5\\ +\,3\\ \hline\end{array}$ $\begin{array}{r}9\\ -\,8\\ \hline\end{array}$ $\begin{array}{r}7\\ +\,2\\ \hline\end{array}$ $\begin{array}{r}8\\ \times\,8\\ \hline\end{array}$ $\begin{array}{r}4\\ +\,9\\ \hline\end{array}$

4 − 1	1)6	7 + 9	9)54	3 + 4	5 + 7	9 + 6	3 × 2	4)20
5)5	5)10	16 − 8	3 × 7	6)48	2 + 6	6 + 2	1)4	8 + 8
3 × 8	4 × 1	9 × 7	3 + 9	6 + 1	7 + 8	4)16	5)25	2 × 3
18 − 9	15 − 9	5 + 1	7 + 5	8 × 4	1 × 5	2)6	9 + 3	7)7
7 − 3	6 + 8	11 − 3	8 + 5	4)4	7)63	6 − 2	7)35	7 − 5
6)12	5)20	1)7	3)27	7 + 4	2 + 3	6)18	3 + 1	1 × 2
9 × 3	8)24	5 × 5	11 − 8	3)24	16 − 9	10 − 5	14 − 8	5 × 2
15 − 7	6 × 4	6 − 3	5 × 6	2)4	8 + 6	14 − 7	7 − 6	5 × 7
9 + 2	4)12	4)36	10 − 3	5 − 2	6 × 1	9 × 8	12 − 8	10 − 1

5 − 3	4 × 7	9 + 6	1 + 4	1 × 6	5 × 5	2)18	3)24	11 − 8
1 × 5	5 + 7	1 + 8	15 − 7	10 − 6	9 × 3	6)6	7 × 2	7 − 6
4 − 3	10 − 5	8 + 9	1 × 2	4 + 7	4 × 3	5 × 7	12 − 9	2)16
4 + 1	7 − 1	8)64	7 + 7	3 × 8	2 + 1	4 + 8	8 + 1	9 + 9
3 × 2	3 + 2	3)15	7 + 5	5 + 3	6)18	6 + 2	9 − 3	7 × 8
7)7	2 + 8	7 − 5	10 − 1	6 × 3	4)24	6)42	2)6	9 − 4
6 − 3	8 + 4	7)21	1)6	11 − 7	2 + 4	13 − 4	9)63	8)56
6 + 5	7 + 6	9 − 5	11 − 3	12 − 5	12 − 4	5)45	5 + 6	3 × 9
8 × 6	9 + 2	6 + 7	12 − 6	7)35	16 − 8	7 × 4	7 + 4	9)27

7 × 1	11 − 2	8)64	9 × 1	3 × 3	5 × 9	6 × 9	1 + 4	3)3
6 + 1	4)32	11 − 6	3)27	1 × 2	11 − 5	15 − 7	3 + 6	4 × 7
18 − 9	7)35	2 × 4	5 × 5	2 × 6	9)72	4)24	7)14	3 + 9
9 × 2	4 − 3	8 × 7	6 + 6	8 − 2	2 + 4	8 − 5	3 + 1	1 + 3
2 + 8	2)10	2 + 6	13 − 4	3)24	12 − 7	4 × 6	5 + 8	4 + 8
8)40	4 + 7	12 − 6	9 − 4	13 − 6	7 + 4	6 + 2	11 − 3	2 × 5
12 − 9	8)24	4)20	8 − 1	6 × 6	5 + 6	6 × 5	3 − 1	8 + 7
7 + 3	1)2	6 × 3	4 + 3	5 + 2	9 × 9	1)5	5 × 7	7 − 2
7)28	9 + 6	5 × 8	7)56	13 − 8	5 + 9	9)54	1 + 7	6)6

Name_____   Date _____ Score _____

3 + 7	9)63	4)24	5)45	1 + 7	15 - 7	6 × 5	8 × 3	8 + 3
7 + 7	4 × 9	4)8	5 × 4	3 + 4	11 - 7	5 + 6	4 + 5	9 × 4
8 × 8	7)21	1)7	3)21	3 × 8	5)30	7)28	7 × 7	3 + 9
12 - 3	4 × 6	5)35	1 + 4	6 + 8	4 + 6	1 + 3	13 - 6	8 × 2
3 - 1	8)48	3)15	14 - 7	16 - 7	2 - 1	9 × 7	9 - 6	6)12
13 - 4	5 × 7	10 - 9	8 × 9	3 + 3	9 + 8	7 × 3	14 - 6	2 × 2
4)4	1 × 4	12 - 4	5 × 6	1 × 6	3)12	5 + 7	2)10	7 + 9
8 + 1	5 + 8	8 × 5	2)6	5 + 3	2 × 7	2 + 2	1 × 2	6 + 2
4)12	7 × 4	7)42	13 - 9	8 × 6	5 + 5	3 + 2	3 × 1	1)5

14

$5)\overline{35}$	$\begin{array}{r}5\\ \times\ 6\\ \hline\end{array}$	$\begin{array}{r}5\\ \times\ 9\\ \hline\end{array}$	$\begin{array}{r}12\\ -\ 6\\ \hline\end{array}$	$\begin{array}{r}3\\ -\ 1\\ \hline\end{array}$	$\begin{array}{r}13\\ -\ 6\\ \hline\end{array}$ $3)\overline{27}$	$3)\overline{3}$	$\begin{array}{r}14\\ -\ 5\\ \hline\end{array}$
$\begin{array}{r}12\\ -\ 7\\ \hline\end{array}$	$\begin{array}{r}2\\ \times\ 5\\ \hline\end{array}$	$\begin{array}{r}4\\ +\ 6\\ \hline\end{array}$	$\begin{array}{r}13\\ -\ 5\\ \hline\end{array}$	$\begin{array}{r}9\\ +\ 4\\ \hline\end{array}$	$\begin{array}{r}7\\ \times\ 2\\ \hline\end{array}$	$\begin{array}{r}12\\ -\ 4\\ \hline\end{array}$	$\begin{array}{r}18\\ -\ 9\\ \hline\end{array}$ $2)\overline{10}$
$\begin{array}{r}3\\ \times\ 8\\ \hline\end{array}$	$\begin{array}{r}6\\ \times\ 3\\ \hline\end{array}$	$\begin{array}{r}16\\ -\ 7\\ \hline\end{array}$	$\begin{array}{r}5\\ +\ 3\\ \hline\end{array}$	$\begin{array}{r}1\\ +\ 1\\ \hline\end{array}$	$\begin{array}{r}6\\ -\ 4\\ \hline\end{array}$	$\begin{array}{r}4\\ +\ 9\\ \hline\end{array}$	$\begin{array}{r}9\\ \times\ 4\\ \hline\end{array}$ $\begin{array}{r}1\\ \times\ 4\\ \hline\end{array}$
$\begin{array}{r}8\\ +\ 6\\ \hline\end{array}$	$\begin{array}{r}1\\ \times\ 6\\ \hline\end{array}$	$\begin{array}{r}4\\ \times\ 8\\ \hline\end{array}$	$\begin{array}{r}7\\ +\ 7\\ \hline\end{array}$	$\begin{array}{r}2\\ +\ 7\\ \hline\end{array}$	$\begin{array}{r}8\\ \times\ 1\\ \hline\end{array}$	$1)\overline{5}$	$\begin{array}{r}10\\ -\ 2\\ \hline\end{array}$ $1)\overline{4}$
$\begin{array}{r}1\\ +\ 9\\ \hline\end{array}$	$1)\overline{8}$	$\begin{array}{r}12\\ -\ 9\\ \hline\end{array}$	$9)\overline{45}$	$\begin{array}{r}2\\ +\ 4\\ \hline\end{array}$	$\begin{array}{r}7\\ +\ 3\\ \hline\end{array}$	$\begin{array}{r}13\\ -\ 9\\ \hline\end{array}$	$\begin{array}{r}3\\ \times\ 3\\ \hline\end{array}$ $\begin{array}{r}8\\ +\ 9\\ \hline\end{array}$
$\begin{array}{r}3\\ +\ 7\\ \hline\end{array}$	$\begin{array}{r}7\\ +\ 1\\ \hline\end{array}$	$\begin{array}{r}6\\ \times\ 7\\ \hline\end{array}$	$\begin{array}{r}10\\ -\ 6\\ \hline\end{array}$	$7)\overline{42}$	$\begin{array}{r}3\\ +\ 5\\ \hline\end{array}$	$7)\overline{49}$	$\begin{array}{r}1\\ \times\ 3\\ \hline\end{array}$ $7)\overline{21}$
$\begin{array}{r}6\\ \times\ 9\\ \hline\end{array}$	$3)\overline{15}$	$\begin{array}{r}5\\ -\ 2\\ \hline\end{array}$	$\begin{array}{r}8\\ +\ 4\\ \hline\end{array}$	$\begin{array}{r}6\\ -\ 5\\ \hline\end{array}$	$\begin{array}{r}5\\ +\ 4\\ \hline\end{array}$	$\begin{array}{r}8\\ +\ 3\\ \hline\end{array}$	$\begin{array}{r}4\\ -\ 2\\ \hline\end{array}$ $9)\overline{9}$
$1)\overline{2}$	$8)\overline{40}$	$\begin{array}{r}5\\ +\ 7\\ \hline\end{array}$	$\begin{array}{r}2\\ +\ 5\\ \hline\end{array}$	$\begin{array}{r}8\\ +\ 7\\ \hline\end{array}$	$\begin{array}{r}3\\ \times\ 1\\ \hline\end{array}$	$2)\overline{8}$	$\begin{array}{r}8\\ +\ 8\\ \hline\end{array}$ $\begin{array}{r}5\\ \times\ 2\\ \hline\end{array}$
$\begin{array}{r}4\\ \times\ 4\\ \hline\end{array}$	$\begin{array}{r}9\\ -\ 7\\ \hline\end{array}$	$\begin{array}{r}7\\ -\ 3\\ \hline\end{array}$	$\begin{array}{r}9\\ -\ 5\\ \hline\end{array}$	$\begin{array}{r}9\\ -\ 3\\ \hline\end{array}$	$4)\overline{16}$	$\begin{array}{r}8\\ \times\ 8\\ \hline\end{array}$	$\begin{array}{r}3\\ \times\ 4\\ \hline\end{array}$ $\begin{array}{r}8\\ -\ 2\\ \hline\end{array}$

6 - 3	6)18	3 × 9	5 × 4	5 × 7	5 + 4	5 × 5	3)9	7 × 4
2)10	1 × 3	7 - 1	8 - 1	1 × 6	6 - 1	8 × 6	4 + 3	6 × 4
5 - 2	10 - 1	7 + 2	8 + 7	5 + 8	2)16	9 - 3	12 - 6	12 - 5
1)4	8)40	8)64	7 × 8	6 + 8	15 - 6	3 + 6	7 - 2	15 - 8
8 × 7	8 + 2	3)12	6)36	1 + 8	8 - 3	8)32	2)8	8 × 2
9 - 6	2 - 1	8 + 9	7)7	16 - 7	8 × 9	1)8	8 × 5	3 - 2
2)18	8 + 1	9)9	3 + 1	5 × 3	1 + 9	1 + 7	7 × 5	9 + 8
7)21	6 × 8	5 + 6	6 + 5	6)24	9 + 2	7 + 5	13 - 4	9 × 5
17 - 9	1 × 5	10 - 6	2 × 2	2 × 9	3)21	1)3	8 - 2	4)28

$8\overline{)32}$ $7\overline{)56}$ $5\overline{)10}$ $\begin{array}{r} 9 \\ + 1 \\ \hline \end{array}$ $7\overline{)49}$ $\begin{array}{r} 11 \\ - 7 \\ \hline \end{array}$ $\begin{array}{r} 4 \\ + 5 \\ \hline \end{array}$ $\begin{array}{r} 17 \\ - 8 \\ \hline \end{array}$ $\begin{array}{r} 1 \\ + 9 \\ \hline \end{array}$

$8\overline{)48}$ $\begin{array}{r} 7 \\ - 6 \\ \hline \end{array}$ $\begin{array}{r} 11 \\ - 4 \\ \hline \end{array}$ $\begin{array}{r} 9 \\ - 4 \\ \hline \end{array}$ $8\overline{)16}$ $\begin{array}{r} 13 \\ - 6 \\ \hline \end{array}$ $\begin{array}{r} 3 \\ + 7 \\ \hline \end{array}$ $1\overline{)7}$ $\begin{array}{r} 10 \\ - 9 \\ \hline \end{array}$

$\begin{array}{r} 8 \\ \times 5 \\ \hline \end{array}$ $\begin{array}{r} 14 \\ - 8 \\ \hline \end{array}$ $\begin{array}{r} 2 \\ \times 3 \\ \hline \end{array}$ $\begin{array}{r} 5 \\ + 3 \\ \hline \end{array}$ $3\overline{)3}$ $\begin{array}{r} 5 \\ \times 7 \\ \hline \end{array}$ $1\overline{)4}$ $\begin{array}{r} 3 \\ + 6 \\ \hline \end{array}$ $\begin{array}{r} 9 \\ - 7 \\ \hline \end{array}$

$\begin{array}{r} 8 \\ + 7 \\ \hline \end{array}$ $5\overline{)30}$ $\begin{array}{r} 3 \\ - 2 \\ \hline \end{array}$ $\begin{array}{r} 7 \\ - 1 \\ \hline \end{array}$ $9\overline{)18}$ $9\overline{)45}$ $\begin{array}{r} 4 \\ + 3 \\ \hline \end{array}$ $7\overline{)21}$ $\begin{array}{r} 2 \\ \times 8 \\ \hline \end{array}$

$\begin{array}{r} 4 \\ + 1 \\ \hline \end{array}$ $3\overline{)9}$ $3\overline{)18}$ $\begin{array}{r} 5 \\ - 2 \\ \hline \end{array}$ $4\overline{)36}$ $\begin{array}{r} 9 \\ \times 2 \\ \hline \end{array}$ $\begin{array}{r} 6 \\ + 8 \\ \hline \end{array}$ $\begin{array}{r} 9 \\ + 2 \\ \hline \end{array}$ $\begin{array}{r} 10 \\ - 4 \\ \hline \end{array}$

$\begin{array}{r} 7 \\ + 8 \\ \hline \end{array}$ $\begin{array}{r} 2 \\ \times 5 \\ \hline \end{array}$ $\begin{array}{r} 6 \\ + 5 \\ \hline \end{array}$ $\begin{array}{r} 1 \\ + 4 \\ \hline \end{array}$ $\begin{array}{r} 8 \\ \times 4 \\ \hline \end{array}$ $5\overline{)15}$ $\begin{array}{r} 16 \\ - 9 \\ \hline \end{array}$ $\begin{array}{r} 1 \\ + 2 \\ \hline \end{array}$ $\begin{array}{r} 18 \\ - 9 \\ \hline \end{array}$

$5\overline{)45}$ $\begin{array}{r} 4 \\ \times 6 \\ \hline \end{array}$ $7\overline{)63}$ $\begin{array}{r} 8 \\ \times 6 \\ \hline \end{array}$ $\begin{array}{r} 2 \\ + 1 \\ \hline \end{array}$ $\begin{array}{r} 12 \\ - 9 \\ \hline \end{array}$ $\begin{array}{r} 6 \\ + 9 \\ \hline \end{array}$ $\begin{array}{r} 2 \\ + 6 \\ \hline \end{array}$ $\begin{array}{r} 6 \\ - 5 \\ \hline \end{array}$

$\begin{array}{r} 2 \\ + 2 \\ \hline \end{array}$ $\begin{array}{r} 7 \\ \times 4 \\ \hline \end{array}$ $9\overline{)72}$ $\begin{array}{r} 1 \\ + 8 \\ \hline \end{array}$ $\begin{array}{r} 13 \\ - 5 \\ \hline \end{array}$ $\begin{array}{r} 6 \\ \times 9 \\ \hline \end{array}$ $\begin{array}{r} 6 \\ - 4 \\ \hline \end{array}$ $\begin{array}{r} 2 \\ \times 7 \\ \hline \end{array}$ $\begin{array}{r} 6 \\ + 6 \\ \hline \end{array}$

$\begin{array}{r} 8 \\ + 8 \\ \hline \end{array}$ $\begin{array}{r} 1 \\ \times 9 \\ \hline \end{array}$ $\begin{array}{r} 9 \\ + 3 \\ \hline \end{array}$ $2\overline{)10}$ $\begin{array}{r} 7 \\ + 2 \\ \hline \end{array}$ $\begin{array}{r} 8 \\ \times 7 \\ \hline \end{array}$ $\begin{array}{r} 7 \\ \times 6 \\ \hline \end{array}$ $\begin{array}{r} 3 \\ + 2 \\ \hline \end{array}$ $\begin{array}{r} 9 \\ \times 9 \\ \hline \end{array}$

4 + 3	2 + 2	4 + 7	5)10	3 - 2	8)72	2 × 4	6 × 8	1 × 6
4)8	6)6	4)4	5 × 1	1 + 8	1)6	7)7	8)24	4 + 8
9 - 1	7 - 2	2 - 1	7)35	4)32	4)36	5 × 4	5 + 9	2 × 3
3 + 5	6)42	1 + 4	7 + 8	7 + 5	4)12	3)15	5 + 6	4 × 6
9 × 5	1 × 3	6 + 6	6)48	8 - 2	6 - 4	5 - 2	3 × 2	6 × 6
4 × 8	12 - 7	8 × 7	9 × 7	6 - 3	2)2	2 + 8	3 + 8	2 × 1
8 × 5	4)20	1)2	2 + 5	7 + 6	7)56	15 - 9	8 × 6	3)6
1 × 7	8 - 5	2 + 9	4)24	11 - 9	8)8	8 + 7	8 + 4	10 - 9
7 × 5	3 × 6	8 × 2	14 - 9	13 - 7	7 + 2	1)8	1 + 6	5)20

1 + 8	1)4	4)12	8)72	3 + 2	5 - 4	13 - 5	6 × 5	8 × 1
9 - 8	9)72	14 - 9	6)36	4 × 4	4 + 2	1 × 8	7 + 3	2 + 9
8 × 8	4 + 6	3 + 1	3 × 3	9)9	8 × 3	8 - 7	7 - 5	8 + 3
8)56	3 + 4	1 × 1	6 + 4	1 × 2	2 + 2	1)1	5 - 2	17 - 9
5 × 5	9 - 7	12 - 7	5 + 4	14 - 7	2)12	10 - 4	4 + 5	3 × 6
13 - 8	8 - 4	1 × 9	2 + 8	6)12	4 + 3	6 × 4	3 × 7	7)7
5 + 8	7 + 2	8 + 9	1 + 6	12 - 3	9)18	2 - 1	14 - 5	3 + 3
9 × 9	3 + 8	2 × 7	4 × 3	9)63	3)15	5 - 3	5 × 6	8 × 9
7 - 4	2 × 4	13 - 7	3 + 6	6 - 5	17 - 8	8 + 7	14 - 6	8 × 2

```
    1        1                    14                4        7                    1
  + 1      + 2     3)18          -  7    3)21     + 7      - 6     2)14         × 6


    5        6        2          2        8        5        8        9            6
  - 3      - 3      + 7        × 2      - 2      × 9      × 2      - 4          - 5


    1        1        6          2                                    10           9
  + 4      × 8      × 6        + 2     1)3     6)30     8)64       -  9         - 3


   10        8        9          5       11        8                  9           12
  -  6     + 1      - 5        × 8      - 9      + 4     4)4        + 3         - 6


             15        3                  4        3        6        9            1
  5)40      -  8      × 1     2)8       + 2      × 8      × 4      × 6          × 1


    3       14        3          5        6        3                 13
  × 5      - 9      + 4        × 6      × 1      + 2     2)12       -  4         1)9


                       7         11
  4)24     1)8       + 2        - 4     7)42     5)30       7        1)6         6)12
                                                         × 4


    8        9                  7        7        4        5       13            6
  × 1      + 7     8)48        × 7      - 4      - 3      - 2      -  6         + 7


    8       15        4                  5                 3        7
  + 3      - 6      × 3     1)2        + 8     1)5       + 8      × 6          4)20
```

$7\overline{)28}$	$\begin{array}{r} 4 \\ \times\ 2 \\ \hline \end{array}$	$\begin{array}{r} 7 \\ -\ 6 \\ \hline \end{array}$	$\begin{array}{r} 5 \\ +\ 8 \\ \hline \end{array}$	$\begin{array}{r} 3 \\ \times\ 5 \\ \hline \end{array}$	$\begin{array}{r} 13 \\ -\ 8 \\ \hline \end{array}$	$\begin{array}{r} 3 \\ \times\ 2 \\ \hline \end{array}$	$\begin{array}{r} 3 \\ +\ 5 \\ \hline \end{array}$	$\begin{array}{r} 4 \\ +\ 5 \\ \hline \end{array}$
$\begin{array}{r} 5 \\ \times\ 9 \\ \hline \end{array}$	$2\overline{)14}$	$6\overline{)42}$	$\begin{array}{r} 1 \\ +\ 6 \\ \hline \end{array}$	$\begin{array}{r} 11 \\ -\ 8 \\ \hline \end{array}$	$5\overline{)40}$	$\begin{array}{r} 4 \\ +\ 6 \\ \hline \end{array}$	$1\overline{)6}$	$\begin{array}{r} 1 \\ +\ 9 \\ \hline \end{array}$
$\begin{array}{r} 18 \\ -\ 9 \\ \hline \end{array}$	$\begin{array}{r} 8 \\ \times\ 3 \\ \hline \end{array}$	$\begin{array}{r} 3 \\ -\ 1 \\ \hline \end{array}$	$\begin{array}{r} 4 \\ -\ 3 \\ \hline \end{array}$	$\begin{array}{r} 7 \\ +\ 5 \\ \hline \end{array}$	$8\overline{)16}$	$\begin{array}{r} 4 \\ \times\ 8 \\ \hline \end{array}$	$\begin{array}{r} 6 \\ \times\ 6 \\ \hline \end{array}$	$\begin{array}{r} 6 \\ +\ 6 \\ \hline \end{array}$
$\begin{array}{r} 7 \\ +\ 1 \\ \hline \end{array}$	$\begin{array}{r} 7 \\ +\ 3 \\ \hline \end{array}$	$\begin{array}{r} 9 \\ \times\ 9 \\ \hline \end{array}$	$\begin{array}{r} 6 \\ -\ 2 \\ \hline \end{array}$	$\begin{array}{r} 5 \\ +\ 5 \\ \hline \end{array}$	$8\overline{)32}$	$\begin{array}{r} 4 \\ \times\ 4 \\ \hline \end{array}$	$\begin{array}{r} 9 \\ +\ 3 \\ \hline \end{array}$	$8\overline{)8}$
$5\overline{)35}$	$\begin{array}{r} 2 \\ +\ 3 \\ \hline \end{array}$	$\begin{array}{r} 17 \\ -\ 9 \\ \hline \end{array}$	$5\overline{)30}$	$\begin{array}{r} 4 \\ +\ 7 \\ \hline \end{array}$	$\begin{array}{r} 14 \\ -\ 9 \\ \hline \end{array}$	$2\overline{)6}$	$3\overline{)3}$	$\begin{array}{r} 6 \\ \times\ 1 \\ \hline \end{array}$
$\begin{array}{r} 9 \\ \times\ 8 \\ \hline \end{array}$	$7\overline{)63}$	$\begin{array}{r} 5 \\ +\ 1 \\ \hline \end{array}$	$\begin{array}{r} 5 \\ +\ 6 \\ \hline \end{array}$	$\begin{array}{r} 8 \\ +\ 3 \\ \hline \end{array}$	$\begin{array}{r} 7 \\ \times\ 4 \\ \hline \end{array}$	$\begin{array}{r} 5 \\ -\ 4 \\ \hline \end{array}$	$7\overline{)7}$	$\begin{array}{r} 11 \\ -\ 2 \\ \hline \end{array}$
$\begin{array}{r} 5 \\ \times\ 1 \\ \hline \end{array}$	$\begin{array}{r} 2 \\ \times\ 6 \\ \hline \end{array}$	$\begin{array}{r} 17 \\ -\ 8 \\ \hline \end{array}$	$\begin{array}{r} 8 \\ +\ 8 \\ \hline \end{array}$	$\begin{array}{r} 4 \\ +\ 4 \\ \hline \end{array}$	$\begin{array}{r} 1 \\ \times\ 7 \\ \hline \end{array}$	$\begin{array}{r} 10 \\ -\ 4 \\ \hline \end{array}$	$\begin{array}{r} 7 \\ -\ 3 \\ \hline \end{array}$	$\begin{array}{r} 5 \\ +\ 4 \\ \hline \end{array}$
$\begin{array}{r} 15 \\ -\ 9 \\ \hline \end{array}$	$\begin{array}{r} 12 \\ -\ 4 \\ \hline \end{array}$	$\begin{array}{r} 9 \\ -\ 2 \\ \hline \end{array}$	$\begin{array}{r} 14 \\ -\ 7 \\ \hline \end{array}$	$\begin{array}{r} 9 \\ \times\ 1 \\ \hline \end{array}$	$\begin{array}{r} 11 \\ -\ 4 \\ \hline \end{array}$	$4\overline{)36}$	$9\overline{)9}$	$\begin{array}{r} 3 \\ \times\ 1 \\ \hline \end{array}$
$8\overline{)64}$	$3\overline{)24}$	$\begin{array}{r} 7 \\ \times\ 1 \\ \hline \end{array}$	$9\overline{)81}$	$\begin{array}{r} 1 \\ \times\ 5 \\ \hline \end{array}$	$6\overline{)48}$	$3\overline{)15}$	$\begin{array}{r} 14 \\ -\ 5 \\ \hline \end{array}$	$4\overline{)8}$

6 - 3	5 + 3	7 - 6	1 × 3	3 × 3	8 × 3	3)15	9 - 1	4 × 6
12 - 9	8)56	7 × 1	10 - 4	7)7	5 × 8	6 - 4	2 + 2	2 × 9
6 - 1	2 × 5	17 - 8	5 - 1	7 × 6	2 + 3	8 × 6	10 - 9	3 × 4
4)36	1)8	8 × 4	2 + 9	6 + 3	8)40	1 × 2	13 - 5	3 + 3
5 - 3	11 - 3	9 × 6	1)1	7)28	8)64	6)6	6 + 8	5 + 9
9 + 2	9 × 8	7 × 5	7 - 4	3)18	6)54	8 × 8	8 + 8	2 + 4
8 × 5	13 - 4	13 - 9	4 × 9	3 + 5	11 - 6	2 × 1	4 + 9	2 + 7
7 + 9	4 × 8	7 + 3	2 + 8	5)40	3 × 8	4)12	6 × 7	6)36
5 + 8	1 + 8	3 × 7	9 + 4	8 + 2	12 - 4	6 × 9	8 + 7	4 - 1

	15	2	8	9		8	5	13
3)27	− 7	× 3	+ 7	+ 9	1)1	+ 4	× 3	− 6

	3		13	12	2		1	2
3)18	+ 6	5)5	− 4	− 5	+ 6	4)12	× 4	+ 1

5	9	6		8	17	3	9	
+ 9	+ 3	× 6	2)4	− 1	− 9	× 5	× 7	3)12

1	8	13		5	9	1		8
+ 6	− 6	− 5	5)35	+ 1	− 2	× 1	9)72	+ 6

	7	4	6		1	7	9	12
7)49	− 2	× 1	× 4	7)35	+ 3	× 6	+ 6	− 7

			9	7	4	6	6	6
9)36	2)16	6)18	+ 8	+ 1	× 8	+ 5	+ 4	× 9

		4		7	2	6		10
8)48	6)30	× 2	5)20	× 5	+ 3	× 5	4)4	− 4

7	3		8	4	10		4	7
+ 8	+ 7	8)32	− 4	× 7	− 2	9)63	+ 8	− 1

13		5	9	9		3	2	
− 9	1)6	− 4	+ 4	× 3	1)5	× 2	+ 8	3)9

| $\begin{array}{r} 8 \\ \times\ 3 \\ \hline \end{array}$ | $6\overline{)54}$ | $3\overline{)3}$ | $\begin{array}{r} 1 \\ +\ 4 \\ \hline \end{array}$ | $\begin{array}{r} 6 \\ -\ 1 \\ \hline \end{array}$ | $\begin{array}{r} 9 \\ \times\ 9 \\ \hline \end{array}$ | $\begin{array}{r} 9 \\ \times\ 4 \\ \hline \end{array}$ | $6\overline{)42}$ | $6\overline{)24}$ |

| $9\overline{)72}$ | $\begin{array}{r} 11 \\ -\ 5 \\ \hline \end{array}$ | $\begin{array}{r} 7 \\ \times\ 9 \\ \hline \end{array}$ | $7\overline{)28}$ | $\begin{array}{r} 2 \\ +\ 5 \\ \hline \end{array}$ | $\begin{array}{r} 12 \\ -\ 4 \\ \hline \end{array}$ | $\begin{array}{r} 2 \\ \times\ 3 \\ \hline \end{array}$ | $5\overline{)45}$ | $6\overline{)6}$ |

| $8\overline{)24}$ | $8\overline{)72}$ | $8\overline{)8}$ | $\begin{array}{r} 4 \\ \times\ 6 \\ \hline \end{array}$ | $\begin{array}{r} 8 \\ \times\ 2 \\ \hline \end{array}$ | $\begin{array}{r} 15 \\ -\ 6 \\ \hline \end{array}$ | $\begin{array}{r} 4 \\ +\ 9 \\ \hline \end{array}$ | $\begin{array}{r} 3 \\ +\ 8 \\ \hline \end{array}$ | $\begin{array}{r} 9 \\ -\ 5 \\ \hline \end{array}$ |

| $\begin{array}{r} 8 \\ \times\ 9 \\ \hline \end{array}$ | $\begin{array}{r} 3 \\ +\ 5 \\ \hline \end{array}$ | $\begin{array}{r} 8 \\ +\ 5 \\ \hline \end{array}$ | $\begin{array}{r} 9 \\ +\ 9 \\ \hline \end{array}$ | $\begin{array}{r} 2 \\ +\ 1 \\ \hline \end{array}$ | $\begin{array}{r} 7 \\ -\ 4 \\ \hline \end{array}$ | $\begin{array}{r} 5 \\ -\ 4 \\ \hline \end{array}$ | $\begin{array}{r} 8 \\ +\ 2 \\ \hline \end{array}$ | $\begin{array}{r} 3 \\ \times\ 1 \\ \hline \end{array}$ |

| $\begin{array}{r} 4 \\ +\ 8 \\ \hline \end{array}$ | $\begin{array}{r} 6 \\ \times\ 4 \\ \hline \end{array}$ | $2\overline{)8}$ | $\begin{array}{r} 1 \\ \times\ 8 \\ \hline \end{array}$ | $3\overline{)6}$ | $\begin{array}{r} 5 \\ +\ 3 \\ \hline \end{array}$ | $\begin{array}{r} 6 \\ \times\ 2 \\ \hline \end{array}$ | $2\overline{)6}$ | $\begin{array}{r} 6 \\ -\ 5 \\ \hline \end{array}$ |

| $8\overline{)48}$ | $\begin{array}{r} 5 \\ -\ 3 \\ \hline \end{array}$ | $\begin{array}{r} 10 \\ -\ 1 \\ \hline \end{array}$ | $\begin{array}{r} 4 \\ +\ 7 \\ \hline \end{array}$ | $\begin{array}{r} 5 \\ +\ 9 \\ \hline \end{array}$ | $\begin{array}{r} 5 \\ \times\ 6 \\ \hline \end{array}$ | $\begin{array}{r} 12 \\ -\ 8 \\ \hline \end{array}$ | $\begin{array}{r} 1 \\ \times\ 1 \\ \hline \end{array}$ | $\begin{array}{r} 4 \\ \times\ 7 \\ \hline \end{array}$ |

| $\begin{array}{r} 9 \\ \times\ 5 \\ \hline \end{array}$ | $3\overline{)18}$ | $\begin{array}{r} 9 \\ \times\ 7 \\ \hline \end{array}$ | $\begin{array}{r} 4 \\ \times\ 2 \\ \hline \end{array}$ | $2\overline{)12}$ | $\begin{array}{r} 15 \\ -\ 7 \\ \hline \end{array}$ | $\begin{array}{r} 8 \\ \times\ 7 \\ \hline \end{array}$ | $\begin{array}{r} 7 \\ \times\ 3 \\ \hline \end{array}$ | $\begin{array}{r} 2 \\ +\ 8 \\ \hline \end{array}$ |

| $\begin{array}{r} 7 \\ +\ 7 \\ \hline \end{array}$ | $\begin{array}{r} 5 \\ \times\ 2 \\ \hline \end{array}$ | $\begin{array}{r} 10 \\ -\ 5 \\ \hline \end{array}$ | $\begin{array}{r} 10 \\ -\ 4 \\ \hline \end{array}$ | $\begin{array}{r} 2 \\ +\ 3 \\ \hline \end{array}$ | $\begin{array}{r} 4 \\ \times\ 8 \\ \hline \end{array}$ | $6\overline{)30}$ | $\begin{array}{r} 7 \\ +\ 3 \\ \hline \end{array}$ | $5\overline{)15}$ |

| $4\overline{)20}$ | $\begin{array}{r} 7 \\ +\ 5 \\ \hline \end{array}$ | $\begin{array}{r} 5 \\ \times\ 3 \\ \hline \end{array}$ | $\begin{array}{r} 8 \\ -\ 3 \\ \hline \end{array}$ | $\begin{array}{r} 3 \\ \times\ 8 \\ \hline \end{array}$ | $\begin{array}{r} 3 \\ -\ 2 \\ \hline \end{array}$ | $\begin{array}{r} 4 \\ -\ 1 \\ \hline \end{array}$ | $\begin{array}{r} 3 \\ +\ 4 \\ \hline \end{array}$ | $\begin{array}{r} 6 \\ \times\ 9 \\ \hline \end{array}$ |

$2\overline{)12}$ $9\overline{)27}$

$$\begin{array}{r}3\\\times\ 8\\\hline\end{array}\qquad\begin{array}{r}4\\+\ 6\\\hline\end{array}\qquad\begin{array}{r}8\\+\ 6\\\hline\end{array}\qquad\begin{array}{r}10\\-\ 4\\\hline\end{array}\qquad\begin{array}{r}2\\\times\ 6\\\hline\end{array}\qquad\begin{array}{r}1\\+\ 6\\\hline\end{array}\qquad\begin{array}{r}2\\+\ 1\\\hline\end{array}$$

$$\begin{array}{r}10\\-\ 6\\\hline\end{array}\qquad\begin{array}{r}6\\\times\ 6\\\hline\end{array}\qquad\begin{array}{r}7\\+\ 4\\\hline\end{array}\qquad\begin{array}{r}8\\\times\ 5\\\hline\end{array}\qquad\begin{array}{r}8\\\times\ 1\\\hline\end{array}\qquad\begin{array}{r}4\\+\ 3\\\hline\end{array}\qquad\begin{array}{r}5\\\times\ 5\\\hline\end{array}\qquad\begin{array}{r}2\\\times\ 1\\\hline\end{array}\qquad\begin{array}{r}7\\+\ 5\\\hline\end{array}$$

$$\begin{array}{r}3\\\times\ 1\\\hline\end{array}\qquad\begin{array}{r}1\\\times\ 7\\\hline\end{array}\qquad\begin{array}{r}4\\\times\ 8\\\hline\end{array}\qquad 2\overline{)10}\qquad\begin{array}{r}5\\-\ 4\\\hline\end{array}\qquad\begin{array}{r}3\\\times\ 7\\\hline\end{array}\qquad 8\overline{)8}\qquad\begin{array}{r}18\\-\ 9\\\hline\end{array}\qquad\begin{array}{r}8\\\times\ 6\\\hline\end{array}$$

$$\begin{array}{r}3\\+\ 4\\\hline\end{array}\qquad\begin{array}{r}9\\-\ 7\\\hline\end{array}\qquad\begin{array}{r}4\\+\ 4\\\hline\end{array}\qquad\begin{array}{r}7\\-\ 5\\\hline\end{array}\qquad\begin{array}{r}2\\\times\ 4\\\hline\end{array}\qquad 7\overline{)42}\qquad\begin{array}{r}6\\+\ 7\\\hline\end{array}\qquad\begin{array}{r}13\\-\ 7\\\hline\end{array}\qquad\begin{array}{r}6\\-\ 3\\\hline\end{array}$$

$$\begin{array}{r}7\\+\ 7\\\hline\end{array}\qquad\begin{array}{r}3\\\times\ 9\\\hline\end{array}\qquad\begin{array}{r}1\\\times\ 8\\\hline\end{array}\qquad\begin{array}{r}2\\\times\ 5\\\hline\end{array}\qquad\begin{array}{r}9\\-\ 3\\\hline\end{array}\qquad\begin{array}{r}5\\+\ 6\\\hline\end{array}\qquad\begin{array}{r}6\\+\ 9\\\hline\end{array}\qquad\begin{array}{r}9\\\times\ 3\\\hline\end{array}\qquad\begin{array}{r}9\\\times\ 2\\\hline\end{array}$$

$$4\overline{)20}\qquad\begin{array}{r}2\\+\ 8\\\hline\end{array}\qquad 8\overline{)72}\qquad\begin{array}{r}6\\\times\ 2\\\hline\end{array}\qquad 2\overline{)18}\qquad\begin{array}{r}3\\\times\ 6\\\hline\end{array}\qquad\begin{array}{r}2\\+\ 4\\\hline\end{array}\qquad\begin{array}{r}10\\-\ 9\\\hline\end{array}\qquad\begin{array}{r}9\\\times\ 5\\\hline\end{array}$$

$$\begin{array}{r}10\\-\ 8\\\hline\end{array}\qquad 5\overline{)35}\qquad\begin{array}{r}9\\-\ 4\\\hline\end{array}\qquad\begin{array}{r}15\\-\ 9\\\hline\end{array}\qquad\begin{array}{r}7\\\times\ 6\\\hline\end{array}\qquad\begin{array}{r}14\\-\ 7\\\hline\end{array}\qquad\begin{array}{r}1\\\times\ 2\\\hline\end{array}\qquad\begin{array}{r}6\\-\ 2\\\hline\end{array}\qquad\begin{array}{r}7\\-\ 6\\\hline\end{array}$$

$$5\overline{)15}\qquad\begin{array}{r}6\\+\ 2\\\hline\end{array}\qquad\begin{array}{r}12\\-\ 3\\\hline\end{array}\qquad\begin{array}{r}3\\+\ 6\\\hline\end{array}\qquad\begin{array}{r}12\\-\ 9\\\hline\end{array}\qquad 7\overline{)35}\qquad\begin{array}{r}1\\+\ 2\\\hline\end{array}\qquad\begin{array}{r}8\\+\ 1\\\hline\end{array}\qquad\begin{array}{r}5\\\times\ 2\\\hline\end{array}$$

$$\begin{array}{r}7\\\times\ 2\\\hline\end{array}\qquad 4\overline{)12}\qquad 5\overline{)40}\qquad 6\overline{)36}\qquad\begin{array}{r}6\\-\ 4\\\hline\end{array}\qquad\begin{array}{r}11\\-\ 3\\\hline\end{array}\qquad\begin{array}{r}13\\-\ 4\\\hline\end{array}\qquad 1\overline{)2}\qquad\begin{array}{r}12\\-\ 4\\\hline\end{array}$$

$$
\begin{array}{ccccccccc}
\begin{array}{r}6\\ \times\,5\end{array} &
8\overline{)48} &
\begin{array}{r}10\\ -\,1\end{array} &
\begin{array}{r}4\\ +\,3\end{array} &
1\overline{)2} &
\begin{array}{r}6\\ +\,7\end{array} &
\begin{array}{r}3\\ +\,6\end{array} &
\begin{array}{r}6\\ \times\,3\end{array} &
\begin{array}{r}2\\ \times\,1\end{array}
\end{array}
$$

$$
\begin{array}{ccccccccc}
\begin{array}{r}1\\ +\,9\end{array} &
\begin{array}{r}2\\ +\,2\end{array} &
9\overline{)27} &
\begin{array}{r}10\\ -\,6\end{array} &
\begin{array}{r}6\\ +\,4\end{array} &
\begin{array}{r}9\\ -\,4\end{array} &
\begin{array}{r}3\\ -\,2\end{array} &
\begin{array}{r}10\\ -\,8\end{array} &
\begin{array}{r}3\\ +\,9\end{array}
\end{array}
$$

$$
\begin{array}{ccccccccc}
\begin{array}{r}4\\ \times\,8\end{array} &
7\overline{)7} &
\begin{array}{r}7\\ +\,5\end{array} &
\begin{array}{r}11\\ -\,9\end{array} &
\begin{array}{r}5\\ \times\,8\end{array} &
9\overline{)63} &
\begin{array}{r}1\\ \times\,4\end{array} &
\begin{array}{r}8\\ +\,2\end{array} &
\begin{array}{r}2\\ +\,7\end{array}
\end{array}
$$

$$
\begin{array}{ccccccccc}
\begin{array}{r}3\\ \times\,3\end{array} &
\begin{array}{r}12\\ -\,4\end{array} &
\begin{array}{r}4\\ +\,4\end{array} &
9\overline{)36} &
\begin{array}{r}4\\ \times\,1\end{array} &
8\overline{)16} &
\begin{array}{r}9\\ \times\,9\end{array} &
\begin{array}{r}9\\ \times\,6\end{array} &
8\overline{)40}
\end{array}
$$

$$
\begin{array}{ccccccccc}
\begin{array}{r}3\\ +\,4\end{array} &
\begin{array}{r}16\\ -\,8\end{array} &
\begin{array}{r}2\\ +\,5\end{array} &
\begin{array}{r}3\\ \times\,2\end{array} &
\begin{array}{r}12\\ -\,8\end{array} &
\begin{array}{r}5\\ \times\,5\end{array} &
\begin{array}{r}8\\ +\,9\end{array} &
\begin{array}{r}5\\ \times\,6\end{array} &
\begin{array}{r}2\\ \times\,2\end{array}
\end{array}
$$

$$
\begin{array}{ccccccccc}
3\overline{)18} &
4\overline{)4} &
\begin{array}{r}1\\ \times\,1\end{array} &
\begin{array}{r}10\\ -\,7\end{array} &
6\overline{)42} &
\begin{array}{r}3\\ \times\,6\end{array} &
\begin{array}{r}1\\ \times\,9\end{array} &
\begin{array}{r}8\\ \times\,3\end{array} &
\begin{array}{r}6\\ \times\,7\end{array}
\end{array}
$$

$$
\begin{array}{ccccccccc}
\begin{array}{r}6\\ -\,5\end{array} &
\begin{array}{r}10\\ -\,2\end{array} &
\begin{array}{r}14\\ -\,7\end{array} &
6\overline{)24} &
\begin{array}{r}4\\ \times\,9\end{array} &
\begin{array}{r}5\\ \times\,2\end{array} &
2\overline{)4} &
\begin{array}{r}1\\ \times\,3\end{array} &
\begin{array}{r}3\\ \times\,1\end{array}
\end{array}
$$

$$
\begin{array}{ccccccccc}
\begin{array}{r}9\\ \times\,1\end{array} &
\begin{array}{r}8\\ -\,3\end{array} &
\begin{array}{r}2\\ \times\,6\end{array} &
\begin{array}{r}9\\ +\,4\end{array} &
\begin{array}{r}10\\ -\,9\end{array} &
\begin{array}{r}5\\ \times\,4\end{array} &
\begin{array}{r}4\\ +\,7\end{array} &
\begin{array}{r}8\\ \times\,6\end{array} &
9\overline{)45}
\end{array}
$$

$$
\begin{array}{ccccccccc}
\begin{array}{r}16\\ -\,7\end{array} &
\begin{array}{r}7\\ +\,8\end{array} &
8\overline{)64} &
4\overline{)32} &
\begin{array}{r}17\\ -\,8\end{array} &
\begin{array}{r}12\\ -\,9\end{array} &
\begin{array}{r}8\\ -\,5\end{array} &
\begin{array}{r}1\\ +\,6\end{array} &
\begin{array}{r}3\\ +\,8\end{array}
\end{array}
$$

$$7\overline{)14} \qquad \begin{array}{r} 6 \\ \times\ 9 \\ \hline \end{array} \qquad 2\overline{)18} \qquad \begin{array}{r} 2 \\ +\ 9 \\ \hline \end{array} \qquad \begin{array}{r} 5 \\ +\ 3 \\ \hline \end{array} \qquad \begin{array}{r} 8 \\ -\ 7 \\ \hline \end{array} \qquad \begin{array}{r} 1 \\ +\ 5 \\ \hline \end{array} \qquad \begin{array}{r} 4 \\ -\ 2 \\ \hline \end{array} \qquad \begin{array}{r} 15 \\ -\ 6 \\ \hline \end{array}$$

$$\begin{array}{r} 9 \\ \times\ 7 \\ \hline \end{array} \qquad \begin{array}{r} 8 \\ +\ 2 \\ \hline \end{array} \qquad 8\overline{)32} \qquad \begin{array}{r} 1 \\ +\ 1 \\ \hline \end{array} \qquad 3\overline{)21} \qquad 5\overline{)10} \qquad \begin{array}{r} 12 \\ -\ 7 \\ \hline \end{array} \qquad 4\overline{)24} \qquad 6\overline{)30}$$

$$\begin{array}{r} 7 \\ \times\ 1 \\ \hline \end{array} \qquad \begin{array}{r} 4 \\ \times\ 8 \\ \hline \end{array} \qquad \begin{array}{r} 3 \\ +\ 7 \\ \hline \end{array} \qquad 4\overline{)8} \qquad \begin{array}{r} 3 \\ +\ 5 \\ \hline \end{array} \qquad \begin{array}{r} 3 \\ +\ 6 \\ \hline \end{array} \qquad \begin{array}{r} 9 \\ +\ 3 \\ \hline \end{array} \qquad \begin{array}{r} 9 \\ +\ 7 \\ \hline \end{array} \qquad \begin{array}{r} 6 \\ +\ 2 \\ \hline \end{array}$$

$$\begin{array}{r} 17 \\ -\ 9 \\ \hline \end{array} \qquad 1\overline{)6} \qquad 8\overline{)40} \qquad \begin{array}{r} 15 \\ -\ 9 \\ \hline \end{array} \qquad \begin{array}{r} 5 \\ \times\ 3 \\ \hline \end{array} \qquad \begin{array}{r} 5 \\ \times\ 7 \\ \hline \end{array} \qquad 7\overline{)28} \qquad 9\overline{)72} \qquad 2\overline{)8}$$

$$\begin{array}{r} 9 \\ \times\ 1 \\ \hline \end{array} \qquad 9\overline{)9} \qquad 2\overline{)12} \qquad \begin{array}{r} 9 \\ -\ 1 \\ \hline \end{array} \qquad \begin{array}{r} 4 \\ \times\ 1 \\ \hline \end{array} \qquad \begin{array}{r} 3 \\ \times\ 9 \\ \hline \end{array} \qquad \begin{array}{r} 7 \\ +\ 6 \\ \hline \end{array} \qquad \begin{array}{r} 4 \\ +\ 3 \\ \hline \end{array} \qquad \begin{array}{r} 9 \\ \times\ 8 \\ \hline \end{array}$$

$$\begin{array}{r} 8 \\ \times\ 4 \\ \hline \end{array} \qquad \begin{array}{r} 12 \\ -\ 9 \\ \hline \end{array} \qquad \begin{array}{r} 7 \\ \times\ 7 \\ \hline \end{array} \qquad 7\overline{)35} \qquad \begin{array}{r} 3 \\ \times\ 6 \\ \hline \end{array} \qquad \begin{array}{r} 5 \\ \times\ 6 \\ \hline \end{array} \qquad \begin{array}{r} 3 \\ \times\ 8 \\ \hline \end{array} \qquad \begin{array}{r} 5 \\ \times\ 4 \\ \hline \end{array} \qquad 6\overline{)18}$$

$$\begin{array}{r} 2 \\ +\ 3 \\ \hline \end{array} \qquad 1\overline{)3} \qquad 8\overline{)48} \qquad \begin{array}{r} 12 \\ -\ 5 \\ \hline \end{array} \qquad 4\overline{)36} \qquad \begin{array}{r} 4 \\ +\ 1 \\ \hline \end{array} \qquad \begin{array}{r} 14 \\ -\ 9 \\ \hline \end{array} \qquad \begin{array}{r} 10 \\ -\ 7 \\ \hline \end{array} \qquad \begin{array}{r} 8 \\ +\ 8 \\ \hline \end{array}$$

$$\begin{array}{r} 3 \\ \times\ 3 \\ \hline \end{array} \qquad 2\overline{)2} \qquad \begin{array}{r} 1 \\ \times\ 9 \\ \hline \end{array} \qquad \begin{array}{r} 5 \\ +\ 4 \\ \hline \end{array} \qquad \begin{array}{r} 9 \\ +\ 4 \\ \hline \end{array} \qquad \begin{array}{r} 8 \\ \times\ 9 \\ \hline \end{array} \qquad \begin{array}{r} 14 \\ -\ 8 \\ \hline \end{array} \qquad \begin{array}{r} 7 \\ \times\ 9 \\ \hline \end{array} \qquad \begin{array}{r} 1 \\ \times\ 8 \\ \hline \end{array}$$

$$\begin{array}{r} 4 \\ \times\ 6 \\ \hline \end{array} \qquad 4\overline{)20} \qquad 5\overline{)15} \qquad 4\overline{)12} \qquad \begin{array}{r} 15 \\ -\ 7 \\ \hline \end{array} \qquad 5\overline{)5} \qquad \begin{array}{r} 8 \\ +\ 1 \\ \hline \end{array} \qquad \begin{array}{r} 4 \\ +\ 7 \\ \hline \end{array} \qquad \begin{array}{r} 1 \\ +\ 2 \\ \hline \end{array}$$

| $4\overline{)12}$ | $6\overline{)24}$ | $\begin{array}{r}4\\+\ 8\\\hline\end{array}$ | $\begin{array}{r}7\\-\ 2\\\hline\end{array}$ | $\begin{array}{r}6\\+\ 6\\\hline\end{array}$ | $\begin{array}{r}9\\-\ 7\\\hline\end{array}$ | $\begin{array}{r}11\\-\ 6\\\hline\end{array}$ | $3\overline{)15}$ | $\begin{array}{r}7\\\times\ 9\\\hline\end{array}$ |

| $\begin{array}{r}1\\+\ 5\\\hline\end{array}$ | $\begin{array}{r}6\\+\ 1\\\hline\end{array}$ | $7\overline{)63}$ | $\begin{array}{r}7\\+\ 6\\\hline\end{array}$ | $\begin{array}{r}6\\\times\ 4\\\hline\end{array}$ | $\begin{array}{r}7\\-\ 3\\\hline\end{array}$ | $\begin{array}{r}5\\\times\ 9\\\hline\end{array}$ | $\begin{array}{r}1\\\times\ 3\\\hline\end{array}$ | $\begin{array}{r}5\\\times\ 8\\\hline\end{array}$ |

| $\begin{array}{r}2\\\times\ 2\\\hline\end{array}$ | $\begin{array}{r}4\\+\ 3\\\hline\end{array}$ | $\begin{array}{r}14\\-\ 7\\\hline\end{array}$ | $\begin{array}{r}9\\\times\ 4\\\hline\end{array}$ | $\begin{array}{r}6\\\times\ 9\\\hline\end{array}$ | $\begin{array}{r}8\\+\ 6\\\hline\end{array}$ | $1\overline{)7}$ | $\begin{array}{r}6\\+\ 4\\\hline\end{array}$ | $\begin{array}{r}13\\-\ 8\\\hline\end{array}$ |

| $\begin{array}{r}7\\\times\ 7\\\hline\end{array}$ | $8\overline{)48}$ | $7\overline{)35}$ | $\begin{array}{r}6\\+\ 2\\\hline\end{array}$ | $\begin{array}{r}2\\\times\ 5\\\hline\end{array}$ | $\begin{array}{r}10\\-\ 7\\\hline\end{array}$ | $\begin{array}{r}10\\-\ 9\\\hline\end{array}$ | $\begin{array}{r}8\\-\ 7\\\hline\end{array}$ | $\begin{array}{r}11\\-\ 9\\\hline\end{array}$ |

| $\begin{array}{r}3\\-\ 2\\\hline\end{array}$ | $\begin{array}{r}8\\\times\ 2\\\hline\end{array}$ | $\begin{array}{r}1\\+\ 6\\\hline\end{array}$ | $\begin{array}{r}5\\+\ 4\\\hline\end{array}$ | $\begin{array}{r}4\\\times\ 8\\\hline\end{array}$ | $\begin{array}{r}7\\-\ 4\\\hline\end{array}$ | $\begin{array}{r}1\\+\ 3\\\hline\end{array}$ | $\begin{array}{r}4\\\times\ 9\\\hline\end{array}$ | $\begin{array}{r}5\\+\ 1\\\hline\end{array}$ |

| $\begin{array}{r}8\\\times\ 5\\\hline\end{array}$ | $1\overline{)8}$ | $6\overline{)6}$ | $\begin{array}{r}6\\-\ 1\\\hline\end{array}$ | $\begin{array}{r}8\\\times\ 4\\\hline\end{array}$ | $\begin{array}{r}4\\\times\ 4\\\hline\end{array}$ | $\begin{array}{r}2\\\times\ 7\\\hline\end{array}$ | $\begin{array}{r}5\\\times\ 7\\\hline\end{array}$ | $4\overline{)24}$ |

| $\begin{array}{r}3\\+\ 2\\\hline\end{array}$ | $\begin{array}{r}7\\+\ 2\\\hline\end{array}$ | $\begin{array}{r}9\\-\ 6\\\hline\end{array}$ | $\begin{array}{r}3\\+\ 5\\\hline\end{array}$ | $\begin{array}{r}9\\-\ 1\\\hline\end{array}$ | $8\overline{)16}$ | $8\overline{)40}$ | $\begin{array}{r}13\\-\ 6\\\hline\end{array}$ | $\begin{array}{r}7\\+\ 1\\\hline\end{array}$ |

| $7\overline{)21}$ | $3\overline{)18}$ | $\begin{array}{r}14\\-\ 9\\\hline\end{array}$ | $\begin{array}{r}8\\+\ 4\\\hline\end{array}$ | $\begin{array}{r}5\\+\ 9\\\hline\end{array}$ | $\begin{array}{r}7\\+\ 8\\\hline\end{array}$ | $\begin{array}{r}14\\-\ 8\\\hline\end{array}$ | $4\overline{)28}$ | $\begin{array}{r}13\\-\ 9\\\hline\end{array}$ |

| $5\overline{)10}$ | $\begin{array}{r}7\\+\ 9\\\hline\end{array}$ | $\begin{array}{r}1\\\times\ 6\\\hline\end{array}$ | $\begin{array}{r}12\\-\ 5\\\hline\end{array}$ | $\begin{array}{r}10\\-\ 5\\\hline\end{array}$ | $\begin{array}{r}8\\\times\ 9\\\hline\end{array}$ | $8\overline{)8}$ | $\begin{array}{r}4\\\times\ 1\\\hline\end{array}$ | $\begin{array}{r}2\\\times\ 6\\\hline\end{array}$ |

Name _____ Date _____ Score _____

9 × 8	4 × 1	1 × 2	5 × 5	8)32	6)42	4 × 7	7 × 2	8)16
6 + 6	1 × 9	3 + 3	5)45	9 + 3	6 + 7	6)18	5)35	4 + 3
2 + 7	13 - 7	7 × 5	4 × 3	8 × 7	2 + 2	4 + 6	9 × 4	9 + 4
6 - 1	1 × 3	6 + 5	6 × 6	16 - 9	9 + 1	6 + 9	10 - 9	10 - 7
7 × 6	2 × 7	7 + 3	17 - 9	8 + 7	3 + 2	11 - 5	2)14	15 - 9
3)3	4 + 1	1 + 6	3)18	14 - 8	2)10	7)42	9)27	7 - 2
12 - 9	8 + 5	2 × 9	6 × 2	6 × 4	1 + 4	9 - 6	4)12	12 - 3
5 - 3	8 × 3	6 - 2	7 × 1	8 × 1	8 × 2	7 - 4	6 + 1	8 × 5
9 - 1	8)24	3 - 2	7 + 1	7 × 9	6)48	9)45	4)8	5 + 1

29

1 ×4	5 −2	14 −9	5 ×1	6 ×6	4 ×6	6)6	8 −4	6 +2
1)9	3 ×6	1 +1	1 +8	6 ×3	1 +4	11 −5	17 −9	9 ×8
11 −7	1)5	3 +9	2 ×9	6 −2	8 ×8	3 +5	14 −8	2 +3
7 ×5	8 +2	3 +3	7 ×8	2)4	4 ×8	8 −2	3)21	6)48
8 −1	13 −8	2)14	9 ×5	5 −4	8 ×1	2 ×1	4)20	5)20
6 +1	13 −6	3)9	12 −3	4 +8	5 ×5	4)24	3 +7	3 −1
11 −2	1)7	18 −9	15 −6	11 −9	14 −5	5 +6	5 +2	6 +8
6)36	7 ×4	1)6	3)18	7 +1	8)56	2 +9	8 ×7	6)30
12 −9	7)42	8 +9	9 +4	9 +5	1 +6	1 ×5	4 +4	7)28

9 + 8	15 - 9	9 - 2	13 - 8	1 + 2	4)12	13 - 6	3 + 6	3 × 2
7 × 1	5)45	9 - 5	8 + 9	8 × 8	9 + 4	9)9	2 + 8	14 - 9
7 × 8	5)10	11 - 9	10 - 7	9 - 1	6)6	4 × 8	4 - 3	7)14
8)8	6 × 2	2)10	3 × 4	9 - 6	1)6	7 × 4	3 × 5	4 + 8
6 + 8	2 × 3	6)12	1)4	2)12	9)72	5)40	5)25	1 × 3
5 × 8	14 - 6	1 × 1	4)16	2)6	2 × 7	8 + 3	8 - 4	2)4
1)7	8 - 5	9 + 6	8)24	3 + 8	4 × 7	9 × 7	7 + 8	12 - 9
9 × 5	3 × 9	3 + 9	3 × 3	9 × 1	1 + 7	5 × 9	12 - 8	3)24
1)5	9 × 3	5)30	3 + 3	7 + 2	7)49	8 × 1	1 × 2	4)20

$3\overline{)12}$ $3\overline{)24}$ $\begin{array}{r}9\\-\ 1\\\hline\end{array}$ $3\overline{)9}$ $\begin{array}{r}2\\\times\ 1\\\hline\end{array}$ $\begin{array}{r}4\\\times\ 5\\\hline\end{array}$ $\begin{array}{r}7\\+\ 7\\\hline\end{array}$ $\begin{array}{r}15\\-\ 9\\\hline\end{array}$ $6\overline{)36}$

$\begin{array}{r}4\\\times\ 6\\\hline\end{array}$ $\begin{array}{r}10\\-\ 7\\\hline\end{array}$ $\begin{array}{r}8\\\times\ 5\\\hline\end{array}$ $\begin{array}{r}8\\+\ 2\\\hline\end{array}$ $\begin{array}{r}3\\\times\ 4\\\hline\end{array}$ $\begin{array}{r}4\\+\ 6\\\hline\end{array}$ $\begin{array}{r}8\\\times\ 7\\\hline\end{array}$ $\begin{array}{r}3\\\times\ 3\\\hline\end{array}$ $\begin{array}{r}8\\-\ 2\\\hline\end{array}$

$5\overline{)10}$ $\begin{array}{r}5\\+\ 5\\\hline\end{array}$ $\begin{array}{r}9\\-\ 3\\\hline\end{array}$ $\begin{array}{r}8\\\times\ 6\\\hline\end{array}$ $\begin{array}{r}4\\\times\ 3\\\hline\end{array}$ $\begin{array}{r}5\\\times\ 3\\\hline\end{array}$ $\begin{array}{r}14\\-\ 6\\\hline\end{array}$ $\begin{array}{r}5\\\times\ 7\\\hline\end{array}$ $1\overline{)3}$

$9\overline{)72}$ $\begin{array}{r}5\\\times\ 9\\\hline\end{array}$ $\begin{array}{r}11\\-\ 2\\\hline\end{array}$ $\begin{array}{r}2\\\times\ 6\\\hline\end{array}$ $\begin{array}{r}6\\-\ 5\\\hline\end{array}$ $\begin{array}{r}8\\\times\ 3\\\hline\end{array}$ $\begin{array}{r}5\\+\ 4\\\hline\end{array}$ $\begin{array}{r}7\\\times\ 4\\\hline\end{array}$ $\begin{array}{r}8\\+\ 7\\\hline\end{array}$

$3\overline{)27}$ $\begin{array}{r}13\\-\ 9\\\hline\end{array}$ $\begin{array}{r}5\\+\ 3\\\hline\end{array}$ $\begin{array}{r}4\\-\ 3\\\hline\end{array}$ $7\overline{)14}$ $\begin{array}{r}5\\-\ 4\\\hline\end{array}$ $6\overline{)6}$ $\begin{array}{r}5\\\times\ 8\\\hline\end{array}$ $\begin{array}{r}5\\+\ 2\\\hline\end{array}$

$\begin{array}{r}10\\-\ 8\\\hline\end{array}$ $\begin{array}{r}5\\\times\ 4\\\hline\end{array}$ $\begin{array}{r}2\\+\ 2\\\hline\end{array}$ $\begin{array}{r}2\\+\ 8\\\hline\end{array}$ $\begin{array}{r}12\\-\ 3\\\hline\end{array}$ $8\overline{)56}$ $\begin{array}{r}11\\-\ 9\\\hline\end{array}$ $\begin{array}{r}4\\\times\ 7\\\hline\end{array}$ $\begin{array}{r}2\\\times\ 8\\\hline\end{array}$

$5\overline{)40}$ $\begin{array}{r}7\\\times\ 2\\\hline\end{array}$ $7\overline{)49}$ $7\overline{)28}$ $\begin{array}{r}8\\+\ 8\\\hline\end{array}$ $\begin{array}{r}5\\-\ 2\\\hline\end{array}$ $9\overline{)63}$ $4\overline{)20}$ $\begin{array}{r}7\\+\ 9\\\hline\end{array}$

$\begin{array}{r}2\\+\ 6\\\hline\end{array}$ $\begin{array}{r}14\\-\ 8\\\hline\end{array}$ $\begin{array}{r}14\\-\ 9\\\hline\end{array}$ $4\overline{)4}$ $5\overline{)20}$ $\begin{array}{r}17\\-\ 9\\\hline\end{array}$ $\begin{array}{r}7\\\times\ 8\\\hline\end{array}$ $\begin{array}{r}13\\-\ 7\\\hline\end{array}$ $\begin{array}{r}6\\+\ 4\\\hline\end{array}$

$\begin{array}{r}6\\\times\ 2\\\hline\end{array}$ $\begin{array}{r}15\\-\ 8\\\hline\end{array}$ $6\overline{)30}$ $\begin{array}{r}1\\+\ 9\\\hline\end{array}$ $\begin{array}{r}8\\+\ 5\\\hline\end{array}$ $\begin{array}{r}9\\+\ 6\\\hline\end{array}$ $\begin{array}{r}10\\-\ 3\\\hline\end{array}$ $\begin{array}{r}7\\+\ 5\\\hline\end{array}$ $\begin{array}{r}6\\\times\ 5\\\hline\end{array}$

8 − 5	6)36	2)16	2 − 1	4)16	7)7	9 − 1	13 − 5	9 × 5
10 − 6	15 − 7	7 − 6	2 + 6	7 × 2	13 − 4	18 − 9	9 × 9	2 + 9
7 + 4	9)18	2 + 5	6 × 8	3)6	8 + 9	9 − 5	2)18	14 − 6
4 + 1	16 − 8	5 + 7	7 + 8	9 × 8	1 + 4	7 + 7	15 − 9	8 + 5
9 + 6	4)4	11 − 5	12 − 6	2 × 3	5)35	4 + 7	6)18	2)8
7)49	1 × 2	10 − 2	7 × 4	3 + 6	9 − 2	3 × 9	6 + 8	12 − 8
1 + 8	5 + 6	6 + 6	6)30	3 × 1	5 + 9	6 + 7	6)42	3 + 1
2 × 5	5 + 5	2)4	1)1	4 + 4	5 × 1	1 + 2	4 + 3	14 − 8
1 + 5	6 × 5	8 + 4	14 − 5	5 + 4	9 − 7	5)45	3)12	6 + 4

33

Name_____ Date _____ Score _____

$2\overline{)12}$ $7\overline{)21}$ $\begin{array}{r}11\\-\ 5\\\hline\end{array}$ $\begin{array}{r}9\\+\ 1\\\hline\end{array}$ $\begin{array}{r}2\\+\ 8\\\hline\end{array}$ $6\overline{)36}$ $\begin{array}{r}3\\\times\ 8\\\hline\end{array}$ $\begin{array}{r}1\\\times\ 2\\\hline\end{array}$ $\begin{array}{r}8\\\times\ 7\\\hline\end{array}$

$\begin{array}{r}11\\-\ 7\\\hline\end{array}$ $9\overline{)45}$ $\begin{array}{r}9\\-\ 6\\\hline\end{array}$ $\begin{array}{r}5\\\times\ 6\\\hline\end{array}$ $\begin{array}{r}1\\\times\ 9\\\hline\end{array}$ $1\overline{)7}$ $\begin{array}{r}9\\\times\ 1\\\hline\end{array}$ $\begin{array}{r}5\\+\ 6\\\hline\end{array}$ $6\overline{)30}$

$5\overline{)45}$ $\begin{array}{r}12\\-\ 7\\\hline\end{array}$ $\begin{array}{r}3\\+\ 3\\\hline\end{array}$ $\begin{array}{r}5\\\times\ 2\\\hline\end{array}$ $7\overline{)7}$ $6\overline{)18}$ $\begin{array}{r}8\\+\ 1\\\hline\end{array}$ $\begin{array}{r}12\\-\ 6\\\hline\end{array}$ $8\overline{)24}$

$2\overline{)8}$ $\begin{array}{r}5\\+\ 8\\\hline\end{array}$ $\begin{array}{r}8\\\times\ 5\\\hline\end{array}$ $5\overline{)10}$ $\begin{array}{r}5\\+\ 1\\\hline\end{array}$ $\begin{array}{r}1\\+\ 4\\\hline\end{array}$ $\begin{array}{r}6\\\times\ 9\\\hline\end{array}$ $\begin{array}{r}6\\\times\ 8\\\hline\end{array}$ $2\overline{)18}$

$\begin{array}{r}13\\-\ 4\\\hline\end{array}$ $\begin{array}{r}6\\-\ 4\\\hline\end{array}$ $\begin{array}{r}5\\+\ 3\\\hline\end{array}$ $\begin{array}{r}5\\+\ 5\\\hline\end{array}$ $\begin{array}{r}13\\-\ 9\\\hline\end{array}$ $9\overline{)27}$ $\begin{array}{r}8\\+\ 4\\\hline\end{array}$ $\begin{array}{r}7\\\times\ 7\\\hline\end{array}$ $\begin{array}{r}10\\-\ 8\\\hline\end{array}$

$\begin{array}{r}2\\\times\ 9\\\hline\end{array}$ $3\overline{)9}$ $\begin{array}{r}4\\\times\ 9\\\hline\end{array}$ $\begin{array}{r}3\\\times\ 3\\\hline\end{array}$ $\begin{array}{r}2\\\times\ 1\\\hline\end{array}$ $\begin{array}{r}14\\-\ 6\\\hline\end{array}$ $\begin{array}{r}8\\-\ 3\\\hline\end{array}$ $\begin{array}{r}3\\+\ 4\\\hline\end{array}$ $\begin{array}{r}7\\+\ 6\\\hline\end{array}$

$\begin{array}{r}7\\\times\ 6\\\hline\end{array}$ $\begin{array}{r}8\\+\ 8\\\hline\end{array}$ $2\overline{)16}$ $\begin{array}{r}7\\+\ 8\\\hline\end{array}$ $\begin{array}{r}9\\-\ 5\\\hline\end{array}$ $\begin{array}{r}7\\\times\ 2\\\hline\end{array}$ $\begin{array}{r}5\\-\ 2\\\hline\end{array}$ $\begin{array}{r}9\\-\ 2\\\hline\end{array}$ $\begin{array}{r}2\\-\ 1\\\hline\end{array}$

$\begin{array}{r}3\\+\ 9\\\hline\end{array}$ $\begin{array}{r}11\\-\ 9\\\hline\end{array}$ $\begin{array}{r}6\\+\ 2\\\hline\end{array}$ $\begin{array}{r}9\\-\ 4\\\hline\end{array}$ $\begin{array}{r}2\\\times\ 5\\\hline\end{array}$ $\begin{array}{r}7\\+\ 9\\\hline\end{array}$ $\begin{array}{r}8\\+\ 6\\\hline\end{array}$ $\begin{array}{r}7\\+\ 3\\\hline\end{array}$ $8\overline{)56}$

$\begin{array}{r}6\\+\ 9\\\hline\end{array}$ $\begin{array}{r}6\\+\ 1\\\hline\end{array}$ $\begin{array}{r}7\\\times\ 4\\\hline\end{array}$ $\begin{array}{r}3\\\times\ 5\\\hline\end{array}$ $\begin{array}{r}5\\\times\ 1\\\hline\end{array}$ $\begin{array}{r}8\\\times\ 3\\\hline\end{array}$ $\begin{array}{r}9\\\times\ 7\\\hline\end{array}$ $1\overline{)5}$ $3\overline{)21}$

34

8 − 6	4 + 6	7)63	4 × 9	7 × 3	16 − 7	11 − 3	4)24	7 − 5
2 × 8	3 × 3	4 × 8	7)35	6 − 5	11 − 8	7 × 8	1 + 5	5)30
9 × 8	3)9	5 − 3	5 + 4	14 − 7	9 − 5	9 × 5	6 × 8	12 − 5
9 + 6	4 × 1	6)6	15 − 6	5 + 5	9 − 8	7)49	2)2	9 × 4
3)18	6)42	9 + 7	6)12	2 × 7	9)27	7)7	1)8	3 × 9
6 + 1	3)24	6 × 3	4 + 2	9 + 4	2 × 9	2 + 8	3 × 8	4 − 3
9 × 7	9 + 2	7 × 4	5 × 3	8 × 1	9)81	6)54	7 + 6	13 − 6
4)32	4 + 7	3 + 6	1 + 8	7 − 1	8 × 9	3 × 5	3 − 2	2 − 1
1 × 5	12 − 8	1 + 2	5)5	1 + 6	7)42	12 − 6	2)14	7 + 9

$8\overline{)32}$	$\begin{array}{r} 2 \\ + 9 \\ \hline \end{array}$	$6\overline{)18}$	$\begin{array}{r} 8 \\ \times 8 \\ \hline \end{array}$	$2\overline{)4}$	$\begin{array}{r} 8 \\ \times 4 \\ \hline \end{array}$	$\begin{array}{r} 6 \\ \times 4 \\ \hline \end{array}$	$\begin{array}{r} 2 \\ + 1 \\ \hline \end{array}$	$3\overline{)21}$

$6\overline{)54}$ $\begin{array}{r} 5 \\ \times 5 \\ \hline \end{array}$ $\begin{array}{r} 8 \\ - 6 \\ \hline \end{array}$ $2\overline{)6}$ $\begin{array}{r} 3 \\ \times 9 \\ \hline \end{array}$ $\begin{array}{r} 7 \\ \times 7 \\ \hline \end{array}$ $\begin{array}{r} 2 \\ \times 5 \\ \hline \end{array}$ $\begin{array}{r} 4 \\ + 9 \\ \hline \end{array}$ $8\overline{)48}$

$\begin{array}{r} 1 \\ \times 1 \\ \hline \end{array}$ $\begin{array}{r} 1 \\ + 3 \\ \hline \end{array}$ $\begin{array}{r} 9 \\ + 4 \\ \hline \end{array}$ $\begin{array}{r} 4 \\ \times 9 \\ \hline \end{array}$ $\begin{array}{r} 3 \\ \times 8 \\ \hline \end{array}$ $\begin{array}{r} 6 \\ - 5 \\ \hline \end{array}$ $\begin{array}{r} 9 \\ + 7 \\ \hline \end{array}$ $\begin{array}{r} 7 \\ + 7 \\ \hline \end{array}$ $\begin{array}{r} 10 \\ - 5 \\ \hline \end{array}$

$\begin{array}{r} 14 \\ - 7 \\ \hline \end{array}$ $\begin{array}{r} 11 \\ - 5 \\ \hline \end{array}$ $9\overline{)81}$ $2\overline{)16}$ $\begin{array}{r} 4 \\ + 5 \\ \hline \end{array}$ $\begin{array}{r} 5 \\ \times 1 \\ \hline \end{array}$ $\begin{array}{r} 3 \\ + 3 \\ \hline \end{array}$ $\begin{array}{r} 5 \\ + 5 \\ \hline \end{array}$ $\begin{array}{r} 3 \\ + 1 \\ \hline \end{array}$

$4\overline{)24}$ $\begin{array}{r} 9 \\ - 7 \\ \hline \end{array}$ $7\overline{)63}$ $\begin{array}{r} 9 \\ \times 5 \\ \hline \end{array}$ $3\overline{)15}$ $3\overline{)18}$ $\begin{array}{r} 3 \\ \times 5 \\ \hline \end{array}$ $\begin{array}{r} 4 \\ + 6 \\ \hline \end{array}$ $\begin{array}{r} 2 \\ + 7 \\ \hline \end{array}$

$\begin{array}{r} 11 \\ - 8 \\ \hline \end{array}$ $5\overline{)5}$ $\begin{array}{r} 8 \\ + 2 \\ \hline \end{array}$ $\begin{array}{r} 10 \\ - 8 \\ \hline \end{array}$ $\begin{array}{r} 8 \\ - 7 \\ \hline \end{array}$ $\begin{array}{r} 6 \\ + 6 \\ \hline \end{array}$ $\begin{array}{r} 8 \\ + 5 \\ \hline \end{array}$ $\begin{array}{r} 14 \\ - 6 \\ \hline \end{array}$ $\begin{array}{r} 7 \\ \times 2 \\ \hline \end{array}$

$\begin{array}{r} 7 \\ - 2 \\ \hline \end{array}$ $\begin{array}{r} 4 \\ + 2 \\ \hline \end{array}$ $\begin{array}{r} 4 \\ \times 7 \\ \hline \end{array}$ $\begin{array}{r} 9 \\ \times 6 \\ \hline \end{array}$ $\begin{array}{r} 7 \\ + 5 \\ \hline \end{array}$ $\begin{array}{r} 7 \\ + 8 \\ \hline \end{array}$ $\begin{array}{r} 3 \\ \times 1 \\ \hline \end{array}$ $\begin{array}{r} 5 \\ \times 8 \\ \hline \end{array}$ $\begin{array}{r} 5 \\ + 9 \\ \hline \end{array}$

$\begin{array}{r} 9 \\ - 4 \\ \hline \end{array}$ $\begin{array}{r} 1 \\ \times 3 \\ \hline \end{array}$ $\begin{array}{r} 8 \\ + 3 \\ \hline \end{array}$ $\begin{array}{r} 1 \\ \times 6 \\ \hline \end{array}$ $6\overline{)36}$ $\begin{array}{r} 7 \\ \times 5 \\ \hline \end{array}$ $\begin{array}{r} 7 \\ + 9 \\ \hline \end{array}$ $\begin{array}{r} 1 \\ + 1 \\ \hline \end{array}$ $\begin{array}{r} 7 \\ - 6 \\ \hline \end{array}$

$\begin{array}{r} 11 \\ - 6 \\ \hline \end{array}$ $3\overline{)27}$ $\begin{array}{r} 5 \\ - 3 \\ \hline \end{array}$ $7\overline{)14}$ $\begin{array}{r} 1 \\ + 4 \\ \hline \end{array}$ $\begin{array}{r} 8 \\ + 4 \\ \hline \end{array}$ $\begin{array}{r} 6 \\ + 2 \\ \hline \end{array}$ $\begin{array}{r} 7 \\ \times 4 \\ \hline \end{array}$ $\begin{array}{r} 6 \\ \times 2 \\ \hline \end{array}$

```
   6        8        6        6        5                          6
 × 7      × 1      × 5      × 2      × 9     8)72    6)42       - 1     8)24
```

```
  12       15        5        1                  7        9       12        1
 - 7      - 6      + 2      × 5     6)36      × 5      + 2      - 8      + 8
```

```
   4                           9        4                10        7       10
 + 1     9)81    9)63       - 7      × 8     1)8       - 7      - 6      - 6
```

```
  10        1        6                 11        4               17        6
 - 3      + 2      + 9     5)15       - 6      × 4     2)8       - 9      - 4
```

```
   7        1        2        3        6        9        5        8        8
 × 4      × 2      × 6      × 3      + 3      + 1      - 1      × 2      × 4
```

```
   6       13       13                  3       15        3               10
 × 8      - 4      - 7     4)12       - 1      - 9      + 2     1)9       - 5
```

```
                  17        7        9                                  13
 2)12      - 8      × 1      + 9     4)28    3)24    6)48       - 5     6)12
```

```
   9        1        4        3       12                 7                 5
 - 6      + 3      × 5      × 9      - 6     4)8       + 3     9)72      × 2
```

```
  11        9        8        5       14        5        8        7        2
 - 2      × 1      - 2      + 9      - 9      + 4      - 6      - 2      + 9
```

4 + 9	7 - 6	16 - 9	4 - 1	4)28	1 + 6	8 - 6	7)63	7 × 4
7 + 7	8 + 1	2 × 6	9 × 4	6 + 9	4 × 1	5 + 2	4 + 2	4 + 7
7 × 2	8)56	11 - 9	8 + 7	4 + 3	1 × 2	7 + 9	8 - 4	5 - 2
11 - 5	5 + 9	9)54	4 - 3	2 + 7	9 + 6	2 + 5	6)36	5)20
9 - 7	2 × 3	3)3	8 - 1	9 - 2	10 - 1	7)35	8 × 5	6 + 3
7 + 5	2 × 5	7 + 4	2 + 4	8 + 8	4)12	5 + 8	4)8	7 + 3
1 × 9	1)2	9 + 4	5 + 4	6 × 8	6 × 1	14 - 8	6 + 2	5 × 7
6 - 3	9 + 3	9 × 1	6)54	7 - 3	5 × 4	7)56	3 × 3	4)24
5 - 4	6)24	7)21	2)4	12 - 7	3)6	2 + 3	4)20	7 - 4

Name _____ Date _____ Score _____

8×9	$13 - 7$	$14 - 5$	$6\overline{)48}$	$12 - 5$	$1 + 6$	$1\overline{)9}$	$5\overline{)20}$	7×6
$4\overline{)20}$	4×9	9×5	$3 + 5$	6×1	2×4	$5 - 3$	$8 - 2$	$6\overline{)18}$
5×6	3×7	1×6	$9\overline{)27}$	5×9	$15 - 7$	$3 + 6$	$12 - 8$	$10 - 7$
$10 - 2$	$4 - 3$	9×4	$12 - 6$	3×8	$4 + 6$	$8\overline{)56}$	$6\overline{)6}$	3×9
$8 - 5$	$8 + 8$	$1 + 7$	$3 + 9$	4×6	7×9	$11 - 6$	$8 + 6$	9×1
$9 - 1$	$4\overline{)8}$	$5 + 8$	$4 + 1$	8×6	$1\overline{)6}$	$16 - 7$	5×4	6×4
$8\overline{)64}$	$4 + 3$	$2 + 1$	$6 + 7$	$7 + 5$	$9 - 4$	1×3	$3\overline{)9}$	$2 + 2$
$7 + 4$	$11 - 4$	9×8	$8 + 4$	2×7	$17 - 8$	$5 + 3$	$16 - 9$	$7 + 3$
$9\overline{)63}$	$8\overline{)8}$	$9 - 5$	$9 + 6$	8×8	$5\overline{)10}$	1×2	$16 - 8$	$9 - 3$

39

5 − 3	7 + 5	15 − 8	9 + 4	4 + 3	11 − 2	7)14	6 × 4	3 + 3
13 − 4	2 + 2	4 × 4	15 − 6	6 × 7	8)24	2 × 5	4 × 2	1 × 4
6 + 2	5 + 4	5 × 5	7)35	1)2	8)8	6 × 5	6)12	9 × 5
2 + 3	12 − 9	4 × 8	6 + 1	11 − 8	2)2	1 × 7	8 + 3	1)7
5 × 1	3 + 2	11 − 5	5)25	5 + 9	2 + 4	9 + 8	2 × 1	2 − 1
7 × 9	11 − 6	3)15	4)32	10 − 7	6 − 3	8 × 2	5)20	8 − 4
6)48	9)36	7 − 4	4 + 5	17 − 8	2)12	4 + 7	8 + 5	7)42
11 − 9	5)40	3 × 1	3 − 2	3 × 5	6 − 2	9)81	4)36	2 × 7
5)15	9 − 8	6 × 9	3)24	9 + 5	3)21	2 × 3	8 − 3	16 − 8

$$
\begin{array}{cc}
3 \\
\times\ 4
\end{array}
\qquad
1\overline{)1}
\qquad
\begin{array}{cc}
3 \\
\times\ 2
\end{array}
\qquad
9\overline{)63}
\qquad
\begin{array}{cc}
10 \\
-\ 8
\end{array}
\qquad
\begin{array}{cc}
4 \\
\times\ 2
\end{array}
\qquad
\begin{array}{cc}
2 \\
\times\ 8
\end{array}
\qquad
\begin{array}{cc}
16 \\
-\ 7
\end{array}
\qquad
\begin{array}{cc}
8 \\
\times\ 6
\end{array}
$$

$$
7\overline{)14}
\qquad
7\overline{)63}
\qquad
2\overline{)4}
\qquad
\begin{array}{cc}
5 \\
\times\ 2
\end{array}
\qquad
\begin{array}{cc}
4 \\
+\ 8
\end{array}
\qquad
\begin{array}{cc}
6 \\
-\ 4
\end{array}
\qquad
\begin{array}{cc}
8 \\
+\ 4
\end{array}
\qquad
\begin{array}{cc}
4 \\
\times\ 8
\end{array}
\qquad
\begin{array}{cc}
9 \\
-\ 2
\end{array}
$$

$$
\begin{array}{cc}
17 \\
-\ 9
\end{array}
\qquad
1\overline{)2}
\qquad
\begin{array}{cc}
3 \\
\times\ 1
\end{array}
\qquad
8\overline{)24}
\qquad
\begin{array}{cc}
7 \\
\times\ 7
\end{array}
\qquad
\begin{array}{cc}
3 \\
\times\ 6
\end{array}
\qquad
\begin{array}{cc}
11 \\
-\ 9
\end{array}
\qquad
\begin{array}{cc}
8 \\
+\ 7
\end{array}
\qquad
\begin{array}{cc}
6 \\
+\ 7
\end{array}
$$

$$
\begin{array}{cc}
11 \\
-\ 3
\end{array}
\qquad
\begin{array}{cc}
9 \\
\times\ 6
\end{array}
\qquad
\begin{array}{cc}
7 \\
-\ 1
\end{array}
\qquad
7\overline{)35}
\qquad
\begin{array}{cc}
12 \\
-\ 4
\end{array}
\qquad
\begin{array}{cc}
3 \\
\times\ 9
\end{array}
\qquad
8\overline{)8}
\qquad
\begin{array}{cc}
2 \\
+\ 9
\end{array}
\qquad
6\overline{)12}
$$

$$
2\overline{)12}
\qquad
\begin{array}{cc}
4 \\
\times\ 3
\end{array}
\qquad
\begin{array}{cc}
3 \\
-\ 1
\end{array}
\qquad
\begin{array}{cc}
13 \\
-\ 4
\end{array}
\qquad
\begin{array}{cc}
8 \\
\times\ 1
\end{array}
\qquad
\begin{array}{cc}
5 \\
-\ 4
\end{array}
\qquad
\begin{array}{cc}
9 \\
+\ 4
\end{array}
\qquad
9\overline{)81}
\qquad
\begin{array}{cc}
4 \\
\times\ 4
\end{array}
$$

$$
\begin{array}{cc}
1 \\
\times\ 5
\end{array}
\qquad
\begin{array}{cc}
12 \\
-\ 8
\end{array}
\qquad
3\overline{)15}
\qquad
\begin{array}{cc}
15 \\
-\ 8
\end{array}
\qquad
\begin{array}{cc}
8 \\
-\ 4
\end{array}
\qquad
\begin{array}{cc}
7 \\
\times\ 1
\end{array}
\qquad
\begin{array}{cc}
7 \\
+\ 1
\end{array}
\qquad
\begin{array}{cc}
7 \\
\times\ 5
\end{array}
\qquad
\begin{array}{cc}
4 \\
+\ 1
\end{array}
$$

$$
\begin{array}{cc}
9 \\
-\ 4
\end{array}
\qquad
\begin{array}{cc}
7 \\
-\ 5
\end{array}
\qquad
\begin{array}{cc}
7 \\
+\ 3
\end{array}
\qquad
\begin{array}{cc}
1 \\
\times\ 2
\end{array}
\qquad
4\overline{)8}
\qquad
\begin{array}{cc}
7 \\
+\ 6
\end{array}
\qquad
\begin{array}{cc}
9 \\
-\ 6
\end{array}
\qquad
\begin{array}{cc}
1 \\
+\ 6
\end{array}
\qquad
8\overline{)32}
$$

$$
\begin{array}{cc}
9 \\
+\ 9
\end{array}
\qquad
\begin{array}{cc}
6 \\
\times\ 3
\end{array}
\qquad
\begin{array}{cc}
12 \\
-\ 5
\end{array}
\qquad
\begin{array}{cc}
4 \\
+\ 3
\end{array}
\qquad
\begin{array}{cc}
8 \\
+\ 5
\end{array}
\qquad
8\overline{)48}
\qquad
\begin{array}{cc}
9 \\
+\ 5
\end{array}
\qquad
\begin{array}{cc}
18 \\
-\ 9
\end{array}
\qquad
\begin{array}{cc}
9 \\
\times\ 2
\end{array}
$$

$$
\begin{array}{cc}
12 \\
-\ 3
\end{array}
\qquad
\begin{array}{cc}
5 \\
+\ 3
\end{array}
\qquad
5\overline{)30}
\qquad
\begin{array}{cc}
16 \\
-\ 9
\end{array}
\qquad
\begin{array}{cc}
1 \\
\times\ 1
\end{array}
\qquad
3\overline{)18}
\qquad
\begin{array}{cc}
8 \\
\times\ 7
\end{array}
\qquad
\begin{array}{cc}
9 \\
+\ 8
\end{array}
\qquad
\begin{array}{cc}
3 \\
\times\ 5
\end{array}
$$

Name_____ Date _____ Score _____

$$\begin{array}{r}7\\+7\\\hline\end{array}\quad\begin{array}{r}8\\\times 4\\\hline\end{array}\quad\begin{array}{r}5\\+1\\\hline\end{array}\quad 7\overline{)14}\quad 2\overline{)8}\quad\begin{array}{r}7\\\times 9\\\hline\end{array}\quad 6\overline{)42}\quad\begin{array}{r}2\\+2\\\hline\end{array}\quad\begin{array}{r}5\\+4\\\hline\end{array}$$

$$2\overline{)18}\quad\begin{array}{r}5\\-3\\\hline\end{array}\quad\begin{array}{r}12\\-8\\\hline\end{array}\quad 8\overline{)72}\quad\begin{array}{r}15\\-9\\\hline\end{array}\quad 3\overline{)15}\quad\begin{array}{r}1\\+1\\\hline\end{array}\quad\begin{array}{r}3\\\times 1\\\hline\end{array}\quad 1\overline{)6}$$

$$\begin{array}{r}9\\-7\\\hline\end{array}\quad 5\overline{)30}\quad\begin{array}{r}8\\\times 7\\\hline\end{array}\quad\begin{array}{r}2\\+7\\\hline\end{array}\quad\begin{array}{r}12\\-6\\\hline\end{array}\quad\begin{array}{r}8\\-5\\\hline\end{array}\quad\begin{array}{r}5\\\times 5\\\hline\end{array}\quad 3\overline{)27}\quad\begin{array}{r}5\\+7\\\hline\end{array}$$

$$\begin{array}{r}8\\+5\\\hline\end{array}\quad\begin{array}{r}3\\\times 5\\\hline\end{array}\quad\begin{array}{r}3\\\times 7\\\hline\end{array}\quad 7\overline{)28}\quad\begin{array}{r}3\\+4\\\hline\end{array}\quad\begin{array}{r}13\\-8\\\hline\end{array}\quad\begin{array}{r}5\\+6\\\hline\end{array}\quad\begin{array}{r}10\\-8\\\hline\end{array}\quad 8\overline{)40}$$

$$\begin{array}{r}9\\\times 2\\\hline\end{array}\quad\begin{array}{r}12\\-9\\\hline\end{array}\quad\begin{array}{r}6\\\times 8\\\hline\end{array}\quad\begin{array}{r}7\\-1\\\hline\end{array}\quad\begin{array}{r}9\\-2\\\hline\end{array}\quad\begin{array}{r}9\\+1\\\hline\end{array}\quad\begin{array}{r}9\\\times 4\\\hline\end{array}\quad\begin{array}{r}5\\+2\\\hline\end{array}\quad\begin{array}{r}6\\+3\\\hline\end{array}$$

$$\begin{array}{r}2\\+6\\\hline\end{array}\quad\begin{array}{r}9\\+3\\\hline\end{array}\quad\begin{array}{r}5\\-2\\\hline\end{array}\quad\begin{array}{r}13\\-4\\\hline\end{array}\quad\begin{array}{r}1\\+8\\\hline\end{array}\quad\begin{array}{r}2\\\times 2\\\hline\end{array}\quad 4\overline{)28}\quad 1\overline{)1}\quad\begin{array}{r}6\\\times 1\\\hline\end{array}$$

$$7\overline{)42}\quad\begin{array}{r}4\\-2\\\hline\end{array}\quad\begin{array}{r}9\\\times 3\\\hline\end{array}\quad\begin{array}{r}7\\+2\\\hline\end{array}\quad\begin{array}{r}9\\+5\\\hline\end{array}\quad\begin{array}{r}14\\-9\\\hline\end{array}\quad 6\overline{)18}\quad\begin{array}{r}4\\\times 6\\\hline\end{array}\quad\begin{array}{r}14\\-8\\\hline\end{array}$$

$$\begin{array}{r}10\\-1\\\hline\end{array}\quad\begin{array}{r}16\\-9\\\hline\end{array}\quad\begin{array}{r}8\\+3\\\hline\end{array}\quad\begin{array}{r}3\\+3\\\hline\end{array}\quad\begin{array}{r}5\\\times 2\\\hline\end{array}\quad 7\overline{)56}\quad\begin{array}{r}4\\+6\\\hline\end{array}\quad\begin{array}{r}9\\+6\\\hline\end{array}\quad 2\overline{)6}$$

$$\begin{array}{r}7\\-3\\\hline\end{array}\quad 5\overline{)10}\quad\begin{array}{r}3\\+2\\\hline\end{array}\quad\begin{array}{r}6\\-1\\\hline\end{array}\quad\begin{array}{r}10\\-2\\\hline\end{array}\quad\begin{array}{r}6\\+1\\\hline\end{array}\quad\begin{array}{r}9\\\times 1\\\hline\end{array}\quad\begin{array}{r}1\\\times 6\\\hline\end{array}\quad\begin{array}{r}4\\\times 5\\\hline\end{array}$$

6 × 3	1 × 4	12 - 7	2 + 2	2 × 8	3 + 5	4 + 5	5)30	3)9

$$6 \times 3 \qquad 1 \times 4 \qquad 12 - 7 \qquad 2 + 2 \qquad 2 \times 8 \qquad 3 + 5 \qquad 4 + 5 \qquad 5\overline{)30} \qquad 3\overline{)9}$$

$$12 - 8 \qquad 4\overline{)24} \qquad 11 - 7 \qquad 15 - 7 \qquad 1\overline{)8} \qquad 4 + 3 \qquad 7\overline{)14} \qquad 9 - 5 \qquad 1 + 3$$

$$12 - 4 \qquad 3 + 2 \qquad 2\overline{)14} \qquad 8 \times 5 \qquad 6 + 6 \qquad 8\overline{)24} \qquad 5 + 8 \qquad 12 - 3 \qquad 7\overline{)21}$$

$$11 - 9 \qquad 12 - 6 \qquad 2 + 7 \qquad 7\overline{)35} \qquad 5 - 4 \qquad 1\overline{)9} \qquad 6 \times 1 \qquad 1 \times 7 \qquad 4 + 6$$

$$5 + 3 \qquad 7 + 7 \qquad 4\overline{)4} \qquad 9 \times 1 \qquad 6\overline{)54} \qquad 9 - 2 \qquad 7 + 2 \qquad 13 - 7 \qquad 5\overline{)40}$$

$$1\overline{)7} \qquad 1 \times 9 \qquad 17 - 8 \qquad 8\overline{)56} \qquad 12 - 5 \qquad 4\overline{)12} \qquad 8 + 1 \qquad 5\overline{)45} \qquad 4\overline{)32}$$

$$6 \times 7 \qquad 2\overline{)4} \qquad 8 + 6 \qquad 8 \times 6 \qquad 8 \times 9 \qquad 4 \times 8 \qquad 1 + 9 \qquad 1 + 5 \qquad 7 + 9$$

$$5 + 1 \qquad 11 - 4 \qquad 4 \times 5 \qquad 4 + 7 \qquad 2 + 6 \qquad 4 \times 3 \qquad 9 + 9 \qquad 9 + 4 \qquad 9 \times 5$$

$$5 + 4 \qquad 3\overline{)21} \qquad 10 - 6 \qquad 5 \times 5 \qquad 4\overline{)16} \qquad 13 - 9 \qquad 7 \times 7 \qquad 7 - 5 \qquad 6 \times 9$$

$9 - 5$	$4 + 2$	$3 - 2$	$8 + 7$	$7 - 1$	$9\overline{)81}$	9×1	$6\overline{)48}$	$8\overline{)72}$
$17 - 8$	$4\overline{)20}$	2×8	$6 + 2$	$2 + 5$	5×8	$1 + 9$	$6 + 1$	7×5
$3\overline{)6}$	$11 - 3$	9×5	$3 + 1$	$9 - 7$	$8\overline{)24}$	$5 + 9$	$14 - 5$	$16 - 9$
6×3	$2\overline{)14}$	$8 + 1$	$13 - 4$	$3\overline{)9}$	$10 - 5$	$5\overline{)20}$	$1\overline{)3}$	$1 + 4$
9×7	$10 - 2$	$5\overline{)25}$	4×4	$1\overline{)9}$	$9 - 6$	$7 - 6$	2×5	$14 - 9$
5×3	$1 + 2$	$15 - 6$	$1\overline{)4}$	8×2	$2 - 1$	$6\overline{)24}$	$5 - 1$	$4\overline{)12}$
$8 + 8$	3×5	$8 - 7$	$11 - 2$	3×4	2×1	$7 + 7$	$3\overline{)18}$	$9 - 8$
$5 + 6$	$1 + 1$	$13 - 5$	4×8	7×2	$2 + 8$	9×6	$5 + 4$	$9 + 7$
$5 - 3$	$4\overline{)36}$	$4\overline{)4}$	5×4	$6\overline{)18}$	$6\overline{)6}$	$14 - 7$	$1\overline{)7}$	4×9

$5\overline{)10}$	$\begin{array}{r}5\\+\,2\\\hline\end{array}$	$\begin{array}{r}1\\\times\,2\\\hline\end{array}$	$\begin{array}{r}5\\+\,7\\\hline\end{array}$	$\begin{array}{r}3\\+\,9\\\hline\end{array}$	$\begin{array}{r}10\\-\,2\\\hline\end{array}$	$\begin{array}{r}2\\\times\,3\\\hline\end{array}$	$3\overline{)24}$	$8\overline{)40}$
$\begin{array}{r}7\\-\,6\\\hline\end{array}$	$\begin{array}{r}7\\-\,5\\\hline\end{array}$	$\begin{array}{r}2\\+\,3\\\hline\end{array}$	$\begin{array}{r}1\\\times\,1\\\hline\end{array}$	$7\overline{)14}$	$\begin{array}{r}12\\-\,7\\\hline\end{array}$	$\begin{array}{r}7\\\times\,1\\\hline\end{array}$	$\begin{array}{r}10\\-\,6\\\hline\end{array}$	$\begin{array}{r}16\\-\,8\\\hline\end{array}$
$\begin{array}{r}6\\+\,3\\\hline\end{array}$	$\begin{array}{r}7\\+\,9\\\hline\end{array}$	$\begin{array}{r}2\\\times\,5\\\hline\end{array}$	$\begin{array}{r}5\\+\,8\\\hline\end{array}$	$1\overline{)7}$	$\begin{array}{r}8\\\times\,7\\\hline\end{array}$	$\begin{array}{r}4\\+\,7\\\hline\end{array}$	$\begin{array}{r}6\\\times\,9\\\hline\end{array}$	$\begin{array}{r}2\\+\,4\\\hline\end{array}$
$\begin{array}{r}9\\\times\,1\\\hline\end{array}$	$3\overline{)3}$	$\begin{array}{r}2\\+\,9\\\hline\end{array}$	$\begin{array}{r}1\\+\,6\\\hline\end{array}$	$\begin{array}{r}14\\-\,9\\\hline\end{array}$	$\begin{array}{r}5\\+\,3\\\hline\end{array}$	$5\overline{)35}$	$5\overline{)30}$	$8\overline{)64}$
$\begin{array}{r}6\\-\,1\\\hline\end{array}$	$\begin{array}{r}8\\+\,8\\\hline\end{array}$	$9\overline{)27}$	$\begin{array}{r}10\\-\,3\\\hline\end{array}$	$7\overline{)42}$	$2\overline{)4}$	$\begin{array}{r}5\\\times\,5\\\hline\end{array}$	$\begin{array}{r}2\\\times\,6\\\hline\end{array}$	$\begin{array}{r}9\\-\,6\\\hline\end{array}$
$\begin{array}{r}7\\+\,4\\\hline\end{array}$	$\begin{array}{r}9\\-\,3\\\hline\end{array}$	$\begin{array}{r}8\\-\,5\\\hline\end{array}$	$\begin{array}{r}11\\-\,8\\\hline\end{array}$	$\begin{array}{r}3\\\times\,3\\\hline\end{array}$	$\begin{array}{r}7\\+\,8\\\hline\end{array}$	$\begin{array}{r}8\\+\,3\\\hline\end{array}$	$\begin{array}{r}3\\+\,4\\\hline\end{array}$	$5\overline{)40}$
$\begin{array}{r}5\\+\,9\\\hline\end{array}$	$\begin{array}{r}8\\-\,4\\\hline\end{array}$	$6\overline{)30}$	$\begin{array}{r}8\\+\,1\\\hline\end{array}$	$\begin{array}{r}7\\+\,3\\\hline\end{array}$	$\begin{array}{r}8\\\times\,1\\\hline\end{array}$	$\begin{array}{r}9\\\times\,2\\\hline\end{array}$	$\begin{array}{r}9\\\times\,5\\\hline\end{array}$	$8\overline{)72}$
$9\overline{)54}$	$7\overline{)49}$	$\begin{array}{r}3\\+\,3\\\hline\end{array}$	$\begin{array}{r}4\\\times\,1\\\hline\end{array}$	$\begin{array}{r}5\\+\,5\\\hline\end{array}$	$\begin{array}{r}8\\+\,9\\\hline\end{array}$	$\begin{array}{r}2\\\times\,2\\\hline\end{array}$	$\begin{array}{r}6\\-\,2\\\hline\end{array}$	$\begin{array}{r}3\\\times\,5\\\hline\end{array}$
$2\overline{)12}$	$6\overline{)48}$	$\begin{array}{r}1\\+\,4\\\hline\end{array}$	$\begin{array}{r}9\\+\,4\\\hline\end{array}$	$\begin{array}{r}8\\\times\,2\\\hline\end{array}$	$\begin{array}{r}16\\-\,7\\\hline\end{array}$	$\begin{array}{r}6\\+\,1\\\hline\end{array}$	$7\overline{)56}$	$\begin{array}{r}1\\\times\,6\\\hline\end{array}$

Name _____ Date _____

BASIC MATH DRILLS

{TIMED TEST}

MULTIPLICATION

If you enjoyed this book. Please check out Basic Math
Drills Timed Test (Multiplication)

Made in the USA
Las Vegas, NV
13 December 2023

82698034R00028